ONE HUNDRED

Bible Stories

In the Words of Holy Scripture

(King James Version)

WITH COLORED ILLUSTRATIONS, SCRIPTURE
PASSAGES, PRAYERS, AND EXPLANATORY NOTES

CONCORDIA PUBLISHING HOUSE

SAINT LOUIS, MISSOURI

Concordia Publishing House, St. Louis, Missouri
Copyright 1950, 1966 by Concordia Publishing House
Library of Congress Catalog Card No. 66-10838
Manufactured in the United States of America
ISBN 0-570-03461-2

5 6 7 8 9 10 11 12 13 14 WP 89 88 87 86 85 84 83 82 81 80

FOREWORD

The selections included in this new edition of ONE HUNDRED BIBLE STORIES have been chosen especially for children ages 9 to 12. Most children of this age have learned to read with ease, and both the King James Bible language and the content of the selections will be within the range of their ability. The book is equally suitable for home or class use.

The main features of this book are:

1. Fifty Old Testament and 50 New Testament stories.
2. A story to a page, with a suitable picture in colors opposite the story, described by a quotation from the text.
3. Most stories of uniform length.
4. Each story told in the words of the Bible (King James Version).
5. Explanatory notes for each story.
6. A pronunciation guide for proper names used in the stories.
7. Direct speech in quotation marks.
8. A Scripture passage and a hymn stanza or prayer opposite each story.
9. A division of the stories into historical periods, in the Table of Contents.
10. Biblical sources of the stories given in the Table of Contents.
11. An effort, in the notes and in the selection of stories, to weave the material into a history and to make this history Christocentric, a history of sin and grace.

Parents and teachers will welcome these features. They should help make the book practical for use in homes and in church agencies such as elementary, Sunday, weekday, and vacation Bible schools.

Most pictures used to illustrate ONE HUNDRED BIBLE STORIES are miniatures of the *Life in Christ Teaching Pictures,* also a Concordia Publishing House product. These large (12¾×17″) teaching pictures can therefore serve as coordinated visual aids during classroom instruction.

The stories in this book necessarily contain only the very essentials. Teachers, parents, and others are therefore urged to read the full Biblical accounts indicated in the Table of Contents. Doing so will help make the Bible itself the main reference and teaching help. Teach the simple text given in this book, but teach it with the understanding and orientation derived from the full Scripture context.

Here are nuggets from the inexhaustible gold mine of the Scriptures, and they are pure gold. May they become the lasting property of many young souls and, by the power of the Holy Spirit, accomplish the purpose for which God has given His Word — repentance, faith, the fear and glory of God, and salvation.

THE PUBLISHER

CONTENTS

THE OLD TESTAMENT

B. The Public Ministry of Christ (About A. D. 29—33)

PARABLES OF THE SAVIOR

C. The Passion and Death of Christ (About A. D. 33)

D. The Glorified Christ (About A. D. 33)

E. The Church of Christ (About A. D. 33—36)

The Old Testament

1. The Creation

The First to the Fourth Day

In the beginning God created[1] the heaven and the earth. And the earth was without form and void,[2] and darkness was upon the face of the deep. And the Spirit of God[3] moved upon the waters.

And God said, "Let there be light." And there was light. And God saw the light, that it was good. And God called the light Day, and the darkness He called Night. And the evening and the morning were the first day.

And God said, "Let there be a firmament[4] in the midst[5] of the waters." And it was so. And God called the firmament Heaven. And the evening and the morning were the second day.

And God said, "Let the waters under the heaven be gathered together unto one place, and let the dry land appear." And it was so. And God called the dry land Earth, and the gathering together of the waters called He Seas. And God saw that it was good.

And God said, "Let the earth bring forth grass, the herb[6] yielding seed and the fruit tree[7] yielding fruit." And it was so. And the earth brought forth grass and herb yielding seed and the fruit tree yielding fruit. And God saw that it was good. And the evening and the morning were the third day.

And God said, "Let there be lights in the firmament of the heaven to give light upon the earth." And God made the greater light[8] to rule the day and the lesser light[9] to rule the night. He made the stars also. And God set them in the firmament of the heaven to give light upon the earth. And God saw that it was good. And the evening and the morning were the fourth day.

Explanatory Notes

[1]Made out of nothing. [2] Empty. [3]Holy Spirit. [4] Sky. [5]To separate waters under the firmament from waters above the firmament. [6]Grains and vegetables. [7]All kinds of trees. [8]Sun. [9]Moon.

"In the beginning"

Bible Text

Our God is in the heavens; He hath done whatsoever He hath pleased. — *Psalm 115:3.*

Hymn

We sing the almighty power of God,
Who bade the mountains rise,
Who spread the flowing seas abroad
And built the lofty skies.

2. The Creation

The Fifth to the Seventh Day

And God said, "Let the waters bring forth abundantly[1] the moving creature that hath life, and fowl[2] that may fly above the earth in the open firmament of heaven." And God created great whales and every living creature that moveth, which the waters brought forth abundantly, and every winged fowl. And God saw that it was good. And God blessed them, saying, "Be fruitful and multiply, and fill the waters in the seas, and let fowl multiply in the earth." And the evening and the morning were the fifth day.

And God said, "Let the earth bring forth the living creature, cattle, and creeping thing, and beast of the earth." And it was so, and God saw that it was good.

And God said, "Let Us[3] make man in Our image,[4] and let them have dominion[5] over the earth."

So God created man in His own image, in the image of God created He him; male[6] and female[7] created He them. And God blessed them and said unto them, "Be fruitful, and multiply,[8] and replenish[9] the earth, and subdue[10] it; and have dominion over the fish of the sea and over the fowl of the air and over every living thing that moveth upon the earth." And God saw everything that He had made, and, behold, it was very good. And the evening and the morning were the sixth day.

Thus the heavens and the earth were finished, and all the host[11] of them. And God rested[12] on the seventh day from all His work which He had made. And God blessed the seventh day and sanctified[13] it.

Explanatory Notes

[1] Plentifully. [2] Birds. [3] Father. Son, and Holy Spirit. [4] Holy like God; a man with a soul, a different and much higher creature than the animals. [5] Rule. [6] Man. [7] Woman. [8] These first parents were to have children and children's children and become the parents of all people in the world. [9] Fill. [10] Make it serve you. [11] Everything in heaven and earth. [12] Stopped creating. [13] Made it a holy day.

"Every living creature"

Bible Text

Through faith we understand that the worlds were framed by the word of God. — *Hebrews 11:3.*

Hymn

From all that dwell below the skies
Let the Creator's praise arise:
   Alleluia! Alleluia!

3. Man and Paradise

And the Lord God formed[1] man of the dust[2] of the ground and breathed into his nostrils the breath of life; and man became a living soul.[3]

And the Lord God planted a garden in Eden,[4] and there He put the man whom He had formed. And out of the ground made the Lord God to grow every tree that is pleasant to the sight and good for food; the tree of life also in the midst of the garden and the tree of knowledge of good and evil. And a river went out of Eden to water the garden. And the Lord God took the man and put him into the Garden of Eden to dress[5] it and to keep it.

And the Lord God commanded the man, saying, "Of every tree of the garden thou mayest freely eat; but of the tree of the knowledge of good and evil, thou shalt not eat of it; for in the day that thou eatest thereof thou shalt surely die."

And the Lord God said, "It is not good that the man should be alone; I will make him an help meet[6] for him." And the Lord God caused a deep sleep to fall upon Adam;[7] and He took one of his ribs and closed up the flesh instead thereof. And the rib which the Lord God had taken from man made He a woman and brought her unto the man.

And Adam said, "This is now bone of my bones and flesh of my flesh. She shall be called Woman because she was taken out of Man." Therefore shall a man leave his father and his mother and shall cleave[8] unto his wife, and they shall be one flesh."[9]

And they were both naked, the man and his wife, and were not ashamed.[10]

Explanatory Notes

[1] Made man's body — this was the sixth day. [2] Earth. [3] Being. [4] E'-den; also called Paradise. [5] Work it. [6] Suitable partner. [7] Ad'-am. [8] Live with her. [9] Like one body, not to be separated — this was the first marriage. [10] Had no sin and therefore no evil thoughts.

"It is not good that the man should be alone"

Bible Text

I will praise Thee, for I am fearfully and wonderfully made. — *Psalm 139:14.*

Hymn

The Lord, my God, be praised,
My Light, my Life, from heaven;
My Maker, who to me
Hath soul and body given.

4. The Fall of Man

Now the serpent[1] was more subtile[2] than any beast of the field which the Lord had made. And he said unto the woman, "Yea, hath God said, 'Ye shall not eat of every tree in the garden'?" [3]

And the woman said unto the serpent, "We may eat of the fruit of the trees of the garden; but of the fruit of the tree which is in the midst of the garden[4] God hath said, 'Ye shall not eat of it, neither shall ye touch it,[5] lest ye die.' "

And the serpent said unto the woman, "Ye shall not surely die; for God doth know that in the day ye eat thereof, then your eyes shall be opened, and ye shall be as gods, knowing good and evil." [6]

And when the woman saw that the tree was good for food, and that it was pleasant to the eyes, and a tree to be desired to make one wise,[7] she took of the fruit thereof and did eat, and gave also unto her husband with her; and he did eat.

And the eyes of them both were opened,[8] and they knew that they were naked. And they sewed fig leaves together and made themselves aprons.

And they heard the voice of the Lord God walking in the garden in the cool of the day.[9] And Adam and his wife hid themselves from the presence of the Lord God among the trees of the garden.[10]

Explanatory Notes

[1] A real snake, through which the devil spoke. [2] Sly and tricky. Satan is a liar, which he showed when, in speaking to the woman, he denied the truth of God's words. [3] This was to raise doubt in the woman's mind. [4] The tree of the knowledge of good and evil. [5] The woman does not give the exact words of God's command. God had said nothing about touching the tree. [6] The devil's words are not true. [7] The woman wanted to be like God; she became proud. [8] They saw the evil they had done. [9] Evening. [10] Because they were afraid of God, fearing death which God had threatened for disobedience.

"She took of the fruit thereof and did eat, and gave also unto her husband with her, and he did eat"

Bible Text

By one man sin entered into the world and death by sin; and so death passed upon all men, for that all have sinned. — *Romans 5:12.*

Hymn

When I'm tempted to do wrong,
Make me steadfast, wise, and strong;
And when all alone I stand,
Shield me with Thy mighty hand.

17

5. The Promise of the Savior

And the Lord God called unto Adam and said unto him, "Where art thou?"

And he said, "I heard Thy voice in the garden, and I was afraid because I was naked; and I hid myself."

And He said, "Who told thee that thou wast naked? Hast thou eaten of the tree whereof I commanded thee that thou shouldest not eat?" [1]

And the man said, "The woman whom Thou gavest to be with me, she gave me of the tree, and I did eat." [2]

And the Lord God said unto the woman, "What is this that thou hast done?"

And the woman said, "The serpent beguiled[3] me, and I did eat."

And the Lord God said unto the serpent, "Because thou hast done this, thou art cursed above every beast of the field. And I will put enmity between thee and the woman, and between thy seed and her Seed; it shall bruise[4] thy head, and thou shalt bruise His heel." [5]

Unto the woman He said, "In sorrow thou shalt bring forth children; and thy desire shall be to thy husband, and he shall rule over thee."

And unto Adam He said, "Cursed is the ground for thy sake. Thorns and thistles shall it bring forth to thee. In the sweat of thy face shalt thou eat bread till thou return unto the ground; for dust thou art, and unto dust shalt thou return." [6]

Unto Adam also and to his wife did the Lord God make coats of skins and clothed them. And He drove out the man;[7] and He placed at the east of the Garden of Eden cherubim, and a flaming sword, which turned every way, to keep the way of the tree of life.[8]

Explanatory Notes

[1] God knows everything. [2] Blames the woman and God, who had given him the woman. [3] Misled. [4] Crush or wound. [5] Jesus had to suffer and die to break the power of the devil. [6] You shall die. [7] With his wife. [8] Paradise on earth was closed.

"And the Lord God called unto Adam and said unto him, 'Where art thou?'"

Bible Text

As by one man's disobedience many were made sinners, so by the obedience of One shall many be made righteous. — *Romans 5:19.*

Hymn

Chief of sinners though I be,
Christ is All in all to me.

6. Cain and Abel[1]

Adam called his wife's name Eve, because she was the mother of all living. And Eve bare Cain, and Abel, his brother. Abel was a keeper of sheep, but Cain was a tiller of the ground.[2]

And it came to pass that Cain brought of the fruit of the ground an offering unto the Lord; and Abel brought of the firstlings[3] of his flock. And the Lord had respect[4] unto Abel and to his offering; but unto Cain and to his offering He had not respect. And Cain was very wroth[5] and his countenance fell.[6]

And the Lord said unto Cain, "Why art thou wroth? If thou doest well, shalt thou not be accepted? If thou doest not well, sin lieth at the door."

And Cain talked with Abel, his brother. And it came to pass, when they were in the field, that Cain rose up against Abel, his brother, and slew[7] him.

And the Lord said unto Cain, "Where is Abel, thy brother?"

And he said, "I know not. Am I my brother's keeper?"

And He said, "What hast thou done? Thy brother's blood crieth unto Me from the ground. And now art thou cursed from the earth, which hath received thy brother's blood from thy hand. The ground shall not henceforth yield unto thee her strength. A fugitive[8] and a vagabond[9] shalt thou be in the earth."

And Cain said unto the Lord, "My punishment is greater than I can bear. Behold, Thou hast driven me out this day, and every one that findeth me shall slay[10] me."

And the Lord set a mark upon Cain lest[11] any finding him should kill him.

Explanatory Notes

[1] A'-bel. [2] Farmer. [3] First-born and best lambs. [4] Liked offering. [5] Very angry. [6] His face showed his anger. [7] Killed. [8] One who flees. [9] One who wanders from place to place. [10] Kill. [11] That not.

"And the Lord had respect unto Abel and to his offering"

Bible Text

Whosoever hateth his brother is a murderer; and ye know that no murderer hath eternal life abiding in him. — *1 John 3:15.*

Hymn

Abel's blood for vengeance
Pleaded to the skies;
But the blood of Jesus
For our pardon cries.

7. From Adam to Noah

Adam lived an hundred and thirty years and begat[1] a son in his own likeness, after his image,[2] and called his name Seth. And the days of Adam, after he had begotten Seth, were eight hundred years, and he begat sons and daughters. And all the days that Adam lived where nine hundred and thirty years; and he died.[3]

Seth begat Enos[4] and other sons and daughters and lived nine hundred and twelve years. Then began men to call upon the name of the Lord.[5]

Enos begat Cainan[6] and other sons and daughters and lived nine hundred and five years.

Cainan begat Mahalaleel[7] and other sons and daughters and lived nine hundred and ten years.

Mahalaleel begat Jared[8] and other sons and daughters and lived eight hundred and ninety-five years.

Jared begat Enoch[9] and other sons and daughters and lived nine hundred and sixty-two years.

Enoch begat Methuselah[10] and other sons and daughters and lived three hundred and sixty-five years. And Enoch walked with God; and he was not,[11] for God took him.

Methuselah begat Lamech[12] and other sons and daughters and lived nine hundred and sixty-nine years.

Lamech begat Noah[13] and other sons and daughters and lived seven hundred and seventy-seven years.

Noah begat Shem, Ham, and Japheth.[14]

Explanatory Notes

[1] Had. [2] Sinful, like Adam, not after the image of God. [3] As God had foretold. [4] E'-nos. [5] Began public worship. [6] Ca-i'-nan. [7] Ma-ha'-la-le-el. [8] Ja'-red. [9] E'-noch. [10] Me-thu'-se-lah. [11] Was no longer seen; it seems God took Enoch to Himself without Enoch first seeing death. [12] La'-mech. [13] No'-ah. [14] Ja'-pheth.

"Then men began to call upon the name of the Lord"

Bible Text

Be fruitful and multiply and replenish the earth. — *Genesis 1:28*

Hymn

Under the shadow of Thy throne
Thy saints have dwelt secure;
Sufficient is Thine arm alone,
And our defense is sure.

8. The Flood

It came to pass when men began to multiply and God saw that the wickedness of man was great, that the Lord said, "I will destroy man from the face of the earth."

But Noah found grace in the eyes of the Lord. He was a just man and walked with God. And God said unto Noah, "Make thee an ark.[1] Behold, I do bring a flood of waters upon the earth. Everything that is in the earth shall die. But with thee will I establish My covenant;[2] and thou shalt come into the ark; thou and thy sons and thy wife and thy sons' wives with thee. And of every living thing shalt thou bring into the ark to keep them alive with thee. And take thou unto thee of all food." Thus did Noah. And the Lord shut him in.

The same day were all the fountains of the great deep[3] broken up, and the windows of heaven were opened.[4] And the rain was upon the earth forty days and forty nights. And the waters increased and the ark went upon the face of the waters; and the mountains were covered. Every living substance[5] was destroyed. And the waters prevailed[6] upon the earth an hundred and fifty days.

And God made a wind to pass over the earth, and the waters assuaged.[7] And the ark rested upon the mountains of Ararat.[8]

And God spake unto Noah, saying, "Go forth of the ark." And Noah went forth, and his sons and his wife and his sons' wives with him, and every beast went forth.

And Noah built an altar unto the Lord and offered burnt offerings. And God blessed Noah and his sons and said unto them, "Be fruitful and multiply and replenish the earth. There shall not any more be a flood to destroy the earth. I do set My bow[9] in the cloud, and it shall be for a token[10] of a covenant between Me and the earth."

Explanatory Notes

[1] Boat. [2] Promise to love and bless Noah. [3] Waters shut up in the earth. [4] It rained as never before or after. [5] Living thing. [6] Remained. [7] Became less. [8] Ar'-a-rat. [9] Rainbow. [10] Sign.

"And Noah built an altar unto the Lord and offered burnt offerings"

Bible Text

Thou art not a God that hath pleasure in wickedness, neither shall evil dwell with Thee. — *Psalm 5:4.*

Prayer

Dear heavenly Father, give us Thy Holy Spirit that we may believe Thy holy Word and lead godly lives; for Jesus' sake. Amen.

9. The Tower of Babel[1]

By the sons of Noah were the nations divided in the earth after the Flood. And the whole earth was of one language and of one speech.[2]

And it came to pass, as they journeyed from the east, that they found a plain; and they dwelt there. And they said one to another, "Go to, let us make brick, and burn[3] them thoroughly." And they had brick for stone, and slime[4] had they for mortar.

And they said, "Go to,[5] let us build us a city and a tower whose top may reach into heaven; and let us make us a name,[6] lest we be scattered abroad upon the face of the whole earth."

And the Lord came down to see the city and the tower which the children of men builded. And the Lord said, "Behold, the people is one, and they have all one language; and this they begin to do. Now, nothing will be restrained[7] from them which they have imagined to do. Go to, let us go down and there confound[8] their language, that they may not understand one another's speech."

So the Lord scattered them abroad from thence[9] upon the face of all the earth; and they left off to build the city. Therefore is the name of it called Babel; because the Lord did there confound the language of all the earth; and from thence did the Lord scatter them abroad upon the face of all the earth.

Explanatory Notes

[1] Ba'-bel, meaning confusion. [2] There was only one language, and all could understand one another and speak to one another. [3] They burned the bricks they made of clay until they were as hard as stone. [4] Soft clay for binding the bricks together. [5] Let us do it. [6] They were proud; the Flood had not destroyed sin; Noah and his children too, were sinners. [7] Held back; they will not be prevented from doing what they have in mind. [8] Confuse, change to many languages. [9] From that place.

"So the Lord scattered them abroad"

Bible Text

He hath showed strength with His arm; He hath scattered the proud in the imagination of their hearts. — *Luke 1:51.*

Prayer

Merciful God, I pray Thee, keep me from vanity and pride; for Jesus' sake. Amen.

10. The Call of Abraham[1]

The Lord said unto Abraham, "Get thee out of thy country and from thy father's house unto a land that I will show thee. And I will make of thee a great nation, and I will bless thee; and in thee shall all families[2] of the earth be blessed." [3]

So Abraham departed, and Lot, his brother's son, went with him; and into the land of Canaan[4] they came. And the Lord appeared unto Abraham and said, "Unto thy seed[5] will I give this land." And there Abraham built an altar and called upon the name of the Lord.[6]

And Lot pitched his tent toward Sodom.[7] But the men of Sodom were wicked before the Lord exceedingly.[8]

After these things the word of the Lord came unto Abraham, saying, "Fear not, Abraham. I am thy Shield[9] and thy great Reward." [10]

And Abraham said, "Lord God, what wilt Thou give me, seeing I go childless?"

And the Lord said, "Look now toward heaven and tell[11] the stars, if thou be able to number them; so shall thy seed be." And he believed in the Lord; and He counted it to him for righteousness.[12]

And when Abraham was ninety years old and nine, the Lord appeared unto him and said, "I am the almighty God; walk before Me,[13] and be thou perfect.[14] And I will establish My covenant between Me and thee and thy seed after thee for an everlasting covenant, to be a God unto thee and to thy seed after thee. This is My covenant: Every man child[15] among you that is eight days old shall be circumcised."

Explanatory Notes

[1] A'-bra-ham, a descendant of Shem. [2] People. [3] In the Savior. [4] Ca'-naan. [5] Children and children's children. [6] Held services with his family and servants. [7] Sod'-om. [8] They were very ungodly. [9] Protector. [10] Having God, Abraham had everything. [11] Count. [12] Abraham knew God to be his Savior; God forgave his sins, and therefore he was just and holy in the sight of God. [13] Walk in the fear of God. [14] Lead a holy life. [15] Boy.

"Look now and tell the stars; so shall thy seed be"

Bible Text

By faith Abraham, when he was called to go out into a place which he should after receive for an inheritance, obeyed; and he went out, not knowing whither he went. — *Hebrews 11:8.*

Prayer

Dear Father in heaven, help me to follow the example of Abraham, who believed and trusted in Thee. Amen.

11. The Promise of Isaac[1]

And the Lord appeared unto Abraham;[2] and he sat in the tent door in the heat of the day.[3] And he lifted up his eyes and looked, and, lo, three men stood by him;[4] and when he saw them, he ran to meet them and bowed himself toward the ground and said, "My Lord, if now I have found favor in Thy sight, pass not away, I pray Thee, from Thy servant. I will fetch a morsel[5] of bread, and comfort ye your hearts.[6] After that ye shall pass on."

And they said, "So do as thou hast said."

And Abraham hastened into the tent unto Sarah[7] and said, "Make ready quickly three measures of fine meal,[8] knead it, and make cakes upon the hearth."[9]

And Abraham ran unto the herd and fetched a calf tender and good, and gave it unto a young man; and he hasted to dress it. And he took butter and milk and the calf which he had dressed and set it before them; and he stood by them under the tree, and they did eat.

And they said unto him, "Where is Sarah, thy wife?"

And he said, "Behold, in the tent."

And He said, "I will certainly return unto thee; and, lo, Sarah, thy wife, shall have a son."

And Sarah heard it in the tent door, which was behind Him, and laughed within herself.[10]

And the Lord said unto Abraham, "Wherefore did Sarah laugh? Is anything too hard for the Lord? At the time appointed[11] I will return unto thee, and Sarah shall have a son."

Then Sarah denied, saying, "I laughed not"; for she was afraid.

And He said, "Nay; but thou didst laugh."

Explanatory Notes

[1] I'-saac. [2] A'-bra-ham. [3] At noon. [4] The Lord and two angels. [5] Small piece. [6] Refresh yourselves. [7] Sa'-rah. [8] Flour. [9] Fireplace. [10] Because it seemed impossible to her that this should happen. [11] At the set time.

"And Sarah heard it in the tent door and laughed"

Bible Text

God is not a man that He should lie. . . . Hath He said, and shall He not do it? Or hath He spoken, and shall He not make it good? — *Numbers 23:19*.

Prayer

Lord, almighty God, Thine is the kingdom and the power and the glory forever. Help me to believe that Thou canst do all things. Amen.

12. Sodom[1] and Gomorrah[2]

And there came two angels[3] to Sodom at even; and Lot sat in the gate of Sodom. And they turned in unto him; and he made them a feast, and they did eat.

But before they lay down, the men of the city of Sodom compassed the house round,[4] both old and young; and they called unto Lot and said, "Where are the men which came in to thee this night? Bring them out unto us that we may know them." [5]

And Lot went out unto them and said, "I pray you, brethren, do not so wickedly."

And they said, "This one fellow came in to sojourn,[6] and he will needs be a judge." [7] And they pressed sore upon Lot[8] and came near to break the door. But the men[9] put forth their hand and pulled Lot into the house to them and shut the door. And they smote the men that were at the door of the house with blindness.

And the men said unto Lot, "Hast thou here any besides? Bring them out of this place; for the Lord hath sent us to destroy it."

And Lot went out and spake unto his sons-in-law; but he seemed as one that mocked unto his sons-in-law.[10] When the morning arose, the angels hastened Lot, saying, "Arise, take thy wife and thy two daughters, lest thou be consumed[11] in the iniquity[12] of the city. Escape for thy life; look not behind thee."

Then the Lord rained upon Sodom and Gomorrah brimstone[13] and fire from the Lord out of heaven. And he overthrew[14] those cities and all the plain and all the inhabitants of the cities. But Lot's wife looked back from behind him, and she became a pillar of salt.

Explanatory Notes

[1] Sod'-om. [2] Go-mor'-rah. [3] The same that visited Abraham. [4] Crowded around the house. [5] Make them join in our ungodly life. [6] To stay a short time. [7] He thinks he is our judge. [8] Tried to force him. [9] The angels. [10] They did not believe him. [11] Eaten up by the fire. [12] Wickedness. [13] Sulphur. [14] Destroyed.

"Lot's wife looked back, and she became a pillar of salt"

Bible Text

The Lord knoweth how to deliver the godly out of temptations and to reserve the unjust unto the Day of Judgment to be punished. — *2 Peter 2:9.*

Prayer

Dear Father in heaven, lead us not into temptation, but deliver us from evil. Amen.

13. The Offering of Isaac[1]

And Sarah[2] bare Abraham[3] a son. And Abraham called the name of his son Isaac and circumcised him.[4]

And God did tempt[5] Abraham and said unto him, "Take now thy son, thine only son Isaac, whom thou lovest, and get thee into the land of Moriah,[6] and offer him there for a burnt offering."

And Abraham rose up and went. On the third day Abraham saw the place afar off. And Abraham took the wood of the burnt offering and laid it upon Isaac; and he took the fire in his hand[7] and a knife; and they went both of them together.

And Isaac said, "My father, behold the fire and the wood; but where is the lamb for a burnt offering?"

Abraham said, "My son, God will provide a lamb for a burnt offering."

And they came to the place; and Abraham built an altar there and laid the wood in order; and bound Isaac, his son, and laid him on the altar upon the wood; and stretched forth his hand and took the knife to slay his son.

And the Angel of the Lord called unto him and said, "Abraham, lay not thine hand upon the lad! For now I know that thou fearest God, seeing thou hast not withheld[8] thine only son from Me." And Abraham lifted up his eyes and saw behind him a ram[9] caught in a thicket[10] by his horns; and he offered him in the stead of his son.

And the Angel of the Lord called unto Abraham out of heaven the second time and said, "By Myself have I sworn, saith the Lord, for because thou hast done this thing, that I will bless thee, and I will multiply thy seed as the stars of heaven; and in thy seed[11] shall all the nations of the earth be blessed."

Explanatory Notes

[1] I'-saac. [2] Sa'-rah. [3] A'-bra-ham. [4] On the eighth day, as God had commanded. [5] Try or test. [6] Mo-ri'-ah. [7] Carried live coals in a vessel. [8] Spared. [9] Male sheep. [10] Bushes. [11] In the Savior, who would be Abraham's descendant.

"Now I know that thou fearest God"

Bible Text

He that loveth son or daughter more than Me is not worthy of Me. — *Matthew 10:37.*

Prayer

Lord, help me to fear Thee, to love Thee, and to trust in Thee in all things; for Jesus' sake. Amen.

14. Isaac[1] Blesses Jacob[2]

Isaac was forty years old when he took Rebekah[3] to wife. And she bare twins. The first was red, all over like a hairy garment; and they called his name Esau.[4] His brother's name was called Jacob. And Isaac loved Esau, but Rebekah loved Jacob.

And when Isaac was old and his eyes were dim, so that he could not see, he called his eldest son and said unto him, "My son, take me some venison[5] and make me savory[6] meat, such as I love, that my soul may bless thee."

And Rebekah heard when Isaac spake to Esau, and she spake unto Jacob, "Go and fetch me two good kids, and I will make them savory meat; and thou shalt bring it to thy father that he may bless thee."[7]

And he went and fetched; and his mother made savory meat. And Rebekah took goodly raiment[8] of Esau and put them upon Jacob; and she put the skins of the kids upon his hands and upon the smooth of his neck.

And he came unto his father and said, "My father!"

And he said, "Who art thou, my son?"

Jacob said, "I am Esau; arise, I pray thee; sit and eat of my venison that thy soul may bless me."

And Isaac said, "Come near that I may feel thee, my son, whether thou be my very son Esau or not." And he felt him and said, "The voice is Jacob's voice, but the hands are the hands of Esau." And he discerned him not[9] and said, "Art thou my very son Esau?"

And he said, "I am."

And he did eat. And Isaac said unto him, "Come near now and kiss me, my son." And he kissed him; and he smelled the smell of his raiment and blessed him and said, "Be lord over thy brethren. Cursed be every one that curseth thee, and blessed be he that blesseth thee."

Explanatory Notes
[1] I'-saac. [2] Ja'-cob. [3] Re-bek'-ah. [4] E'-sau. [5] Meat of game animals. [6] Good-tasting. [7] She knew Jacob was to receive the blessing. [8] Clothes. [9] Did not recognize him.

"Isaac blessed him"

Bible Text

By faith Isaac blessed Jacob and Esau concerning things to come. — *Hebrews 11:20.*

Prayer

Dear Jesus, help us to be truthful and honest in all things, and let Thy will be done among us. Amen.

15. Jacob's Ladder

Jacob[1] was scarce gone out from the presence of his father, when Esau[2] came in from his hunting. And his father said unto him, "Who art thou?" And he said, "I am thy son, thy first-born,[3] Esau." Isaac[4] said, "Thy brother came and hath taken away thy blessing." Esau said, "Bless me also!" And he wept. Isaac answered, "Behold, thy dwelling shall be the fatness of the earth. By thy sword shalt thou live and shalt serve thy brother." [5]

And Esau hated Jacob because of the blessing and said, "I will slay my brother Jacob." And Rebekah[6] called Jacob and said, "Flee thou to Laban,[7] my brother." And Isaac called Jacob and said unto him, "God Almighty bless thee and give thee the blessing of Abraham."

And Jacob went out and lighted[8] upon a certain place and lay down to sleep. And he dreamed, and, behold, a ladder set up on the earth, and the top of it reached to heaven; and, behold, the angels of God ascending[9] and descending[10] on it. And the Lord stood above it and said, "I am the Lord God of Abraham and the God of Isaac; the land whereon thou liest, to thee will I give it, and to thy seed. In thee and in thy seed shall all the families of the earth be blessed."

And Jacob awaked out of his sleep and said, "How dreadful[11] is this place! This is the house of God, and this is the gate of heaven." And Jacob took the stone and set it up for a pillar[12] and poured oil upon the top of it. And he called the name of that place Bethel.[13] And Jacob vowed a vow,[14] saying, "If God will be with me and will keep me, so that I come again to my father's house, then shall the Lord be my God, and this stone shall be God's house."

Explanatory Notes

[1] Ja'-cob. [2] E'-sau. [3] Esau sold his birthright; he had despised it. [4] I'-saac. [5] Esau's descendants should live in plenty, defeat other nations, but serve Jacob's descendants. [6] Re-bek'-ah. [7] La'-ban. [8] Came. [9] Going up. [10] Coming down. [11] God's presence filled Jacob with fear and reverence. [12] Marker. [13] Beth'-el. [14] Promised solemnly.

"The angels of God ascending and descending"

Bible Text

Verily, verily, I say unto you, Hereafter ye shall see heaven open and the angels of God ascending and descending upon the Son of Man. — *John 1:51.*

Prayer

Dear Father in heaven, send Thy holy angels to go with us and to guard us against all danger. Amen.

16. Jacob's Family

And Jacob[1] came to Laban[2] and served him fourteen years for his daughters Leah[3] and Rachel;[4] and after this he served him six years more for cattle; and Jacob increased exceedingly. And the Lord said unto Jacob, "Return unto the land of thy fathers and to thy kindred,[5] and I will be with thee." Then Jacob set his sons and his wives upon camels and came unto Isaac,[6] his father, in Canaan.[7]

The sons of Jacob were twelve: Reuben,[8] Simeon,[9] Levi,[10] Judah,[11] Dan, Naphtali,[12] Gad, Asher,[13] Issachar,[14] Zebulun,[15] Joseph,[16] and Benjamin.[17]

Joseph, being seventeen years old, was feeding the flock with his brethren; and Joseph brought unto his father their evil report.[18] Now, Israel[19] loved Joseph more than all his children, and he made him a coat of many colors. And when his brethren saw this, they hated him and could not speak peaceably unto him.

Joseph dreamed a dream, and he told it his brethren and said, "Hear this dream which I have dreamed: We were binding sheaves[20] in the field, and, lo, my sheaf arose and also stood upright; and your sheaves stood round about and made obeisance[21] to my sheaf."

And his brethren said to him, "Shalt thou indeed reign[22] over us?" And they hated him yet more.

And he dreamed another dream and told his brethren, "I have dreamed the sun, the moon, and eleven stars made obeisance to me."

And his father rebuked[23] him and said, "Shall I and thy mother and thy brethren indeed come to bow down ourselves to thee?" And his brethren envied him; but his father observed[24] the saying.

Explanatory Notes

[1] Ja'-cob. [2] La'-ban. [3] Le'-ah. [4] Ra'-chel. [5] Relatives. [6] I'-saac. [7] Ca'-naan. [8] Reu'-ben. [9] Sim'-e-on. [10] Le'-vi. [11] Ju'-dah. [12] Naph'-ta-li. [13] Ash'-er. [14] Is'-sa-char. [15] Zeb'-u-lun. [16] Jo'-seph. [17] Ben'-ja-min. [18] Told him of their evil deeds. [19] Is'-ra-el, or Jacob. [20] Bundles of grain. [21] Bowed. [22] Rule. [23] Scolded. [24] Remembered.

"And he made him a coat of many colors"

Bible Text

Blessed is everyone that feareth the Lord, that walketh in His ways. — *Psalm 128:1.*

Hymn

In every home bestow Thy grace
On children, father, mother.
Let them together dwell in peace
And love to one another.

41

17. Joseph[1] and His Brethren[2]

And Joseph's brethren went to feed their father's flock in Shechem.[3] And Israel[4] said unto Joseph, "Go, I pray thee, see whether it be well with thy brethren and well with the flocks."

And when they saw him afar off, they said one to another, "Behold, this dreamer cometh. Let us slay him, and we will say, 'Some evil beast hath devoured him'; and we shall see what will become of his dreams." And Reuben[5] heard it, and he delivered him out of their hands and said, "Shed no blood, but cast him into this pit."[6]

When Joseph was come unto his brethren, they stripped him out of his coat of many colors and cast him into a pit; and the pit was empty; there was no water in it. And they sat down to eat bread. And, behold, a company of merchantmen came with their camels. And Judah[7] said, "Come and let us sell our brother." And they lifted up Joseph out of the pit and sold him to the Ishmaelites[8] for twenty pieces of silver.[9] And they brought Joseph into Egypt.[10]

And Reuben returned unto the pit; and, behold, Joseph was not in the pit; and he rent[11] his clothes and returned unto his brethren and said, "The child is not; and I, whither shall I go?"[12] And they took Joseph's coat and killed a kid of the goats and dipped the coat in the blood; and they sent it to their father and said, "This have we found; know now whether it be thy son's coat."

And he knew it and said, "It is my son's coat; an evil beast hath devoured him; Joseph is without doubt rent in pieces." And Jacob mourned for his son many days and refused to be comforted; and he said, "For I will go down into the grave unto my son mourning."[13]

Explanatory Notes
[1] Jo'-seph. [2] Brothers [3] She'-chem. [4] Is'-ra-el. [5] Reu'-ben. [6] Hole; dry cistern or well. [7] Ju'-dah. [8] Ish'-ma-el-ites. [9] Price of a young slave. [10] E'-gypt. [11] Tore. [12] As the first-born he was responsible for Joseph's welfare. [13] He felt he would die of grief.

"They sold Joseph for twenty pieces of silver"

Bible Text

Where envying and strife is, there is confusion and every evil work. — *James 3:16.*

Prayer

Dear Jesus, help us to love our parents and brothers and sisters, and to treat them kindly. Amen.

18. Joseph[1] in Egypt[2]

The Midianites[3] sold Joseph into Egypt unto Potiphar,[4] an officer of Pharaoh[5] and captain of the guard. And the Lord was with Joseph, and the Lord made all that he did to prosper[6] in his hand. And Potiphar made him overseer over his house.

And Joseph was a goodly person and well-favored.[7] And his master's wife cast her eyes upon Joseph; and she said, "Lie with me."

But he refused and said unto her, "How can I do this great wickedness, and sin against God?"

And when his lord came home, she spake unto him, saying, "The Hebrew[8] servant came in unto me to mock[9] me." And Potiphar's wrath was kindled, and he put him into the prison.

But the Lord was with Joseph and gave him favor in the sight of the keeper of the prison; and he committed to Joseph's hand all the prisoners.[10]

And the butler[11] of the king and his baker had offended their lord. And Pharaoh was wroth[12] against them and put them into the prison where Joseph was bound. And they dreamed a dream, both of them, in one night. And Joseph came in unto them and asked them, "Wherefore look ye so sadly today?"

And they said, "We have dreamed a dream, and there is no interpreter[13] of it."

And Joseph said unto them, "Do not interpretations belong to God? Tell me them, I pray you."

And they told him their dreams; and he interpreted them. And as he interpreted to them, so it was.

Explanatory Notes

[1] Jo'-seph. [2] E'-gypt. [3] Mid'-i-an-ites; the merchantmen who had bought Joseph from his brethren. [4] Pot'-i-phar. [5] Pha'-raoh. [6] To be successful. [7] Good-looking. [8] He'-brew. [9] Put me to shame. [10] Made Joseph their overseer. [11] A servant in charge of food and drink. [12] Angry. [13] One who can tell what dreams mean.

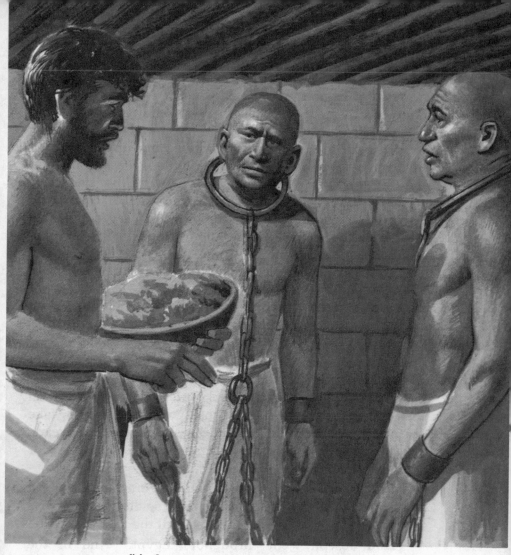

"As he interpreted to them, so it was"

Bible Text

The fear of the Lord is the beginning of wisdom. — *Psalm 111:10.*

Prayer

Dear Lord, guard us and keep us that we may not be led into sin and shame by the devil, the world, or our own sinful heart. Amen.

19. Joseph[1] Before Pharaoh[2]

And it came to pass at the end of two full years that Pharaoh dreamed; and, behold, he stood by the river. And there came up out of the river seven well-favored kine[3] and fat-fleshed. And seven other kine came up, ill-favored[4] and lean-fleshed; and they did eat up the seven well-favored and fat kine. So Pharaoh awoke. And he slept and dreamed the second time; and seven ears of corn came up upon one stalk, rank[5] and good. And seven thin and blasted[6] ears sprung up after them. And in the morning Pharaoh sent for all the magicians[7] in Egypt and told them his dreams; but there was none that could interpret them. Then Pharaoh sent and called Joseph. And Joseph answered, "It is not in me; God shall give Pharaoh an answer of peace." And Pharaoh told Joseph his dreams.

And Joseph said, "The dream of Pharaoh is one. Behold, there come seven years of great plenty throughout all the land of Egypt, and after them seven years of famine.[8] Now, therefore, let Pharaoh look out[9] a man discreet[10] and wise and set him over the land of Egypt; and let him take up the fifth part of the land in the seven plenteous years, that food shall be for store[11] against the seven years of famine."

And Pharaoh said unto Joseph, "Forasmuch as God hath showed thee all this, there is none so discreet and wise as thou art. See, I have set thee over all the land of Egypt."

And Joseph went throughout Egypt. And in the plenteous years he gathered up all the food, very much, until he left numbering.[12] And the years of dearth[13] began to come; and the dearth was in all lands, but in Egypt there was bread.

Explanatory Notes

[1] Jo'-seph. [2] Pha'-raoh. [3] Good-looking cows. [4] Poor-looking. [5] Large. [6] Withered. [7] People who do supernatural things with the help of Satan. [8] General shortage of food. [9] Find. [10] Careful. [11] Stored up. [12] Counting. [13] Great shortage of food.

"And Pharaoh said, 'I have set thee over all the land of Egypt'"

Bible Text
The Lord upholdeth the righteous. — *Psalm 37:17.*

Prayer
Dear Father in heaven, help us to obey Thee and our parents, and grant us such blessings as are good for us; for Jesus' sake. Amen.

20. The First Journey of Joseph's[1] Brethren

Now, when Jacob[2] saw that there was corn in Egypt,[3] he said unto his sons, "Behold, there is corn in Egypt; get you down thither,[4] and buy for us that we may live and not die." And Joseph's ten brethren went down. And they came and bowed themselves before Joseph. And Joseph knew his brethren, but they knew not him.

And Joseph said unto them, "Ye are spies."

And they said, "Nay, my lord, but to buy food are thy servants come. We are true men; thy servants are no spies. We are twelve brethren. The youngest is this day with our father, and one is not."

And Joseph said unto them, "Send one of you, and let him fetch your brother, and ye shall be kept in prison, that your words may be proved." And he put them all together into ward [5] three days.

And Joseph said unto them the third day, "If ye be true men, let one of your brethren be bound in prison. Go ye, but bring your youngest brother unto me; so shall your words be verified." [6]

And they said one to another, "We are verily guilty concerning our brother, in that we saw the anguish of his soul and we would not hear; therefore is this distress come upon us. And they knew not that Joseph understood them; for he spake unto them by an interpreter.[8]

And he turned himself about from them and wept. Then he took from them Simeon[9] and bound him before their eyes. And Joseph commanded to fill their sacks with corn; and they departed thence.

And they came unto their father and told him all that befell unto them. And Jacob said, "Benjamin[10] shall not go down with you; if mischief[11] befall him, then shall ye bring down my gray hairs with sorrow to the grave."

"Ye are spies"

Bible Text

Know and see that it is an evil thing and bitter that thou hast forsaken the Lord, thy God. — *Jeremiah 2:19.*

Prayer

Merciful God, make us sorry for our sins and keep us in Thy grace; for Jesus' sake. Amen.

21. The Second Journey of Joseph's[1] Brethren

Jacob[2] said to his sons, "Go again, buy us a little food."

And Judah[3] said, "The man did solemnly protest[4] unto us, saying, 'Ye shall not see my face except your brother be with you.' Therefore send the lad with me; I will be surety[5] for him."

And their father said unto them, "If it must be so now, do this. And God Almighty give you mercy before the man!"

And they rose up and went down to Egypt and stood before Joseph. And Joseph said to the ruler of his house, "Bring these men home, for they shall dine with me."

And the man did so, and he brought Simeon[6] out unto them.

And when Joseph came home, he asked them of their welfare and said, "Is your father well? Is he yet alive?"

And they answered, "Our father is in good health; he is yet alive."

And he saw his brother Benjamin[7] and said, "Is this your younger brother?" And he said, "God be gracious unto thee, my son."

And Joseph entered into his chamber[8] and wept there. And he washed his face and went out and refrained[9] himself and said, "Set on bread." And they sat before him, the first-born according to his birthright and the youngest according to his youth; and the men marveled[10] one at another. And he took and sent messes[11] unto them from before him; but Benjamin's mess was five times so much as any of theirs.

And Joseph commanded the steward of his house, saying, "Fill the men's sacks with food and put my silver cup in the sack's mouth of the youngest." And he did according to the word that Joseph had spoken.

Explanatory Notes

[1] Jo'-seph. [2] Ja'-cob. [3] Ju'-dah. [4] He insisted. [5] Responsible. [6] Sim'-e-on. [7] Ben'-ja-min. [8] Room. [9] Kept from weeping. [10] Wondered at being seated according to their age. [11] Food for their meal.

"And they sat before him"

Bible Text

This is My commandment: That ye love one another, as I have loved you. — *John 15:12.*

Prayer

Gracious Father in heaven, help us to love Thee and one another, and make us kind and forgiving; for Jesus' sake. Amen.

22. Joseph[1] Makes Himself Known

When the men were gone out of the city, Joseph said unto his steward, "Up, follow the men and say unto them. 'Wherefore have ye rewarded evil for good? Is not this it in which my lord drinketh? Ye have done evil.'" And he overtook them and spake unto them these same words.

And they said unto him, "With whom the cup be found, let him die, and we will be my lord's bondmen."[2]

And he said, "He with whom it is found shall be my servant, and ye shall be blameless." And the cup was found in Benjamin's[3] sack. Then they rent their clothes[4] and returned to the city.

And Joseph said unto them, "What deed is this ye have done? The man in whose hand the cup is found, he shall be my servant."

Then Judah[5] came near unto him and said, "O my lord, when I come to my father and the lad be not with us, we shall bring down the gray hairs of our father with sorrow to the grave. I became surety for the lad; therefore let me abide[6] instead of the lad."

Then Joseph could not refrain himself and wept aloud and said unto his brethren, "I am Joseph; doth my father yet live?"

And his brethren could not answer him; for they were troubled at his presence.

And Joseph said, "Come near me. I am Joseph, whom ye sold into Egypt. Be not grieved, nor angry with yourselves, for God sent me before you to save your lives.[7] Go up to my father and say unto him, 'Thus saith thy son Joseph, "God hath made me lord of all Egypt; come down unto me, tarry not;[8] I will nourish thee."'[9] Haste and bring down my father hither." And he fell upon Benjamin's neck and wept; moreover, he kissed all his brethren.

Explanatory Notes

[1] Jo'-seph. [2] Slaves. [3] Ben'-ja-min. [4] Tore their outer clothes to show their fright and grief. [5] Ju'-dah. [6] Stay. [7] Joseph understood God's plan. [8] Do not wait. [9] Care for you.

"I am Joseph"

Bible Text

Forbearing one another and forgiving one another if any man have a quarrel against any; even as Christ forgave you, so also do ye. — *Colossians 3:13*.

Prayer

Lord, forgive us our sins, as we forgive those who sin against us. Amen.

23. Jacob[1] in Egypt[2]

And Joseph[3] gave his brethren wagons and provisions[4] for the way. To all of them he gave changes of raiment; [5] but to Benjamin he gave three hundred pieces of silver[6] and five changes of raiment. So he sent his brethren away and said, "See that ye fall not out by the way." [7]

And they came into the land of Canaan,[8] unto Jacob, their father, and told him, "Joseph is yet alive, and he is governor over all the land of Egypt." But he believed them not. Then they told him all the words of Joseph. And when he saw the wagons which Joseph had sent to carry him, he said, "It is enough; Joseph, my son, is yet alive; I will go and see him before I die."

And Israel[9] took his journey to Egypt with all that he had. And he sent Judah before him unto Joseph. And Joseph made ready his chariot [10] and went up to meet his father; and he fell on his neck and wept a good while. And Israel said unto Joseph, "Now let me die since I have seen thy face, because thou art yet alive." And Joseph brought Jacob, his father, before Pharaoh; and Jacob blessed Pharaoh. And Joseph nourished his father and his brethren in the land of Egypt with bread; and they had possessions therein and grew and multiplied exceedingly.[11]

And the time drew nigh that Israel must die, and he called his sons together and blessed them; [12] and he was gathered unto his people. And when Joseph's brethren saw that their father was dead, they sent a messenger unto Joseph, saying, "Forgive the trespass of thy brethren and their sin; for they did unto thee evil."

And Joseph wept and said, "As for you, ye thought evil against me; but God meant it unto good." And he comforted them and spake kindly unto them.

Explanatory Notes

[1] Ja'-cob. [2] E'-gypt. [3] Jo'-seph. [4] Food for man and beast. [5] Complete outfit of clothes. [6] As a special sign of brotherly love. [7] Do not quarrel. [8] Ca'-naan. [9] Is'-ra-el. [10] A two-wheeled royal wagon. [11] Grew to large numbers. [12] Judah received the blessing of the Savior. Genesis 49:8-12.

"And Joseph went up to meet his father"

Bible Text

Honor thy father and mother . . . that it may be well with thee
and thou mayest live long on the earth. — *Ephesians 6:2-3.*

Hymn

Give to thy parents honor due,
Be dutiful and loving, too,
And help them when their strength decays;
So shalt thou have length of days.
  Have mercy, Lord!

24. The Birth of Moses[1]

Now, there arose up a new king over Egypt[2] which knew not Joseph.[3] And he said unto his people, "Behold, the people of the children of Israel[4] are more and mightier than we. Let us deal wisely with them."[5]

And they set over them taskmasters[6] to afflict them with their burdens. But the more they afflicted them, the more they multiplied. And Pharaoh charged[7] his people, saying, "Every son that is born ye shall cast into the river."

And a woman of the house of Levi bare a son; and she hid him three months. And she took an ark of bulrushes[8] and daubed it with slime[9] and with pitch[10] and put the child therein; and she laid it in the flags[11] by the river's brink.[12] And his sister stood afar off to wit[13] what would be done to him.

And the daughter of Pharaoh came down to wash herself at the river. When she saw the ark among the flags, she sent her maid to fetch it. And when she had opened it, she saw the child, and, behold, the babe wept. And she had compassion on him.

Then said his sister, "Shall I call a nurse of the Hebrew[14] women?" Pharaoh's daughter said to her, "Go."

And the maid called the child's mother. And Pharaoh's daughter said unto her, "Take this child away, and nurse it for me, and I will give thee thy wages." And the woman took the child and nursed it. And the child grew, and she brought him unto Pharaoh's daughter, and he became her son. And she called his name Moses.

When Moses was grown, he spied an Egyptian smiting[15] a Hebrew. And he slew the Egyptian. Now, when Pharaoh heard this thing, he sought to slay Moses. But Moses fled from the face of Pharaoh.

Explanatory Notes

[1] Mo'-ses. [2] E'-gypt. [3] Jo'-seph. [4] Is'-ra-el. [5] Hold them down. [6] Cruel overseers. [7] Commanded. [8] Tall water grass. [9] Moist, sticky clay. [10] Black, sticky substance. [11] Plants with long, sword-shaped leaves. [12] Bank. [13] Learn. [14] He'-brew. [15] Beating.

"She had compassion on him"

Bible Text

By faith Moses, when he was come to years, refused to be called the son of Pharaoh's daughter, choosing rather to suffer affliction with the people of God than to enjoy the pleasures of sin for a season. — *Hebrews 11:24-25.*

Prayer

Lord, almighty God, defend me against all danger and guard and protect me from all evil; for Jesus' sake. Amen.

25. The Call of Moses[1]

Now, Moses came to the mountain of God, even to Horeb.[2] And the Angel of the Lord appeared unto him in a flame of fire out of the midst of a bush; and the bush was not consumed.[3] And the Lord called unto him and said, "I have seen the affliction[4] of My people in Egypt.[5] Come now, therefore, and I will send thee unto Pharaoh,[6] that thou mayest bring forth My people out of Egypt."

And Moses said, "Who am I that I should go unto Pharaoh and that I should bring forth the children of Israel[7] out of Egypt?" He said, "Certainly I will be with thee."

And Moses answered, "But, behold, they will not believe me."

And the Lord said, "What is that in thine hand?" And he said, "A rod." And He said, "Cast it on the ground." And he cast it on the ground, and it became a serpent; and Moses fled from it. And the Lord said, "Take it by the tail" And he put forth his hand and caught it, and it became a rod in his hand.

And the Lord said furthermore, "Put now thine hand into thy bosom." And he put his hand into his bosom; and when he took it out, behold, his hand was leprous[8] as snow. And He said, "Put it into thy bosom again." And he put it in again; and, behold, it was turned again as his other flesh. "If they will not believe these two signs, thou shalt take of the water of the river and pour it upon dry land; and the water shall become blood."

And Moses said, "O my Lord, but I am slow of speech and of a slow tongue." And the Lord said, "Go, and I will teach thee what thou shalt say." He said, "O my Lord, send, I pray thee, by the hand of him whom thou wilt send." And the anger of the Lord was kindled, and He said, "Is not this Aaron, thy brother? He can speak well. He shall be thy spokesman unto the people." And Moses went.

Explanatory Notes
[1] Mo'-ses. [2] Ho'-reb. [3] Burned. [4] Trouble. [5] E'-gypt. [6] Pha'-raoh. [7] Is'-ra-el. [8] Leprosy is a destructive disease of the skin.

"And the Lord called unto him out of the bush"

Bible Text

Thou shalt go to all that I shall send thee, and whatsoever I command thee thou shalt speak. Be not afraid of their faces, for I am with thee to deliver thee, saith the Lord. — *Jeremiah 1:7-8.*

Prayer

Lord, make me ready to do Thy will at all times. Amen.

26. Moses[1] Before Pharaoh.[2] — The Passover[3]

And afterward Moses and Aaron[4] went in and told Pharaoh, "Thus saith the Lord God of Israel,[5] 'Let My people go.'"

And Pharaoh said, "Who is the Lord that I should obey His voice? I know not the Lord, neither will I let Israel go. Get you unto your burdens!"[6] And Pharaoh did evil to this people.

And Moses and Aaron went in unto Pharaoh; and they showed the miracles as the Lord had commanded. And He hardened Pharaoh's heart that he hearkened not unto them.

And the Lord brought nine plagues[7] upon Pharaoh and the Egyptians;[8] but Pharaoh hardened his heart and refused to let the people go. And the Lord said unto Moses, "Yet will I bring one plague more upon Pharaoh and upon Egypt; afterwards he will let you go hence. Speak ye unto all the congregation of Israel, saying, 'Take every man a lamb without blemish;[9] and ye shall kill it in the evening. And they shall take of the blood and strike it on the two sideposts and on the upper doorpost of the houses; and they shall eat the flesh in that night, roasted with fire, and unleavened[10] bread. And ye shall let nothing of it remain until the morning. And thus shall ye eat it: with your loins girded,[11] your shoes on your feet, and your staff in your hand; and ye shall eat in haste, for it is the Lord's Passover. For I will pass through the land of Egypt this night and will smite all the first-born, both man and beast. And the blood shall be to you for a token[12] upon the houses; when I see the blood, I will pass over you, and the plague shall not be upon you. And this day ye shall keep a feast to the Lord throughout your generations.'"

And the children of Israel did as the Lord had commanded.

Explanatory Notes

[1] Mo'-ses. [2] Pha'-raoh. [3] A festival which was to be a type of Christ. [4] Aa'-ron. [5] Is'-ra-el. [6] Work. [7] Terrible punishments of God. [8] E-gyp'-tians. [9] Fault. [10] Made without yeast. [11] With a belt around a loose garment, ready to travel. [12] Sign.

"When I see the blood, I will pass over you"

Bible Text

Christ, our Passover, is sacrificed for us. — *1 Corinthians 5:7.*

Hymn

How sweet the name of Jesus sounds
    In a believer's ear!
It soothes his sorrows, heals his wounds,
    And drives away his fear.

27. The Departure from Egypt[1]

And at midnight the Lord smote all the first-born in the land of Egypt. And there was a great cry in Egypt; for there was not a house where there was not one dead.

And Pharaoh[2] called for Moses[3] and Aaron[4] by night and said, "Rise up and get you forth from among my people." And the Egyptians were urgent upon the people that they might send them out of the land in haste; for they said, "We be all dead men."

And the children of Israel[5] went out of the land of Egypt, about six hundred thousand on foot that were men, besides children. And the Lord went before them by day in a pillar of a cloud, to lead them the way; and by night in a pillar of fire, to give them light.

And it was told the king of Egypt that the people fled; and he pursued after them and overtook them encamping by the sea. And the children of Israel were sore afraid and cried out unto the Lord.

And Moses said unto the people, "Fear not; the Lord shall fight for you." And the Angel of God removed and went behind them; and the pillar of the cloud came between the camp of the Egyptians and the camp of Israel. And Moses stretched out his hand over the sea; and the waters were divided. And the children of Israel went into the midst of the sea upon the dry ground; and the waters were a wall unto them on their right hand and on their left.

And the Egyptians pursued and went in after them. And the Lord troubled the host of the Egyptians and took off their chariot[6] wheels, so that the Egyptians said, "Let us flee, for the Lord fighteth for them."

And the Lord said unto Moses, "Stretch out thine hand over the sea." And the sea returned and covered all the host of Pharaoh; there remained not one of them.

Explanatory Notes

[1] E'-gypt. [2] Pha'-raoh. [3] Mo'-ses. [4] Aa'-ron. [5] Is'-ra-el. [6] Two-wheeled wagon.

"And Moses stretched out his hand over the sea"

Bible Text

By faith they passed through the Red Sea as by dry land; which the Egyptians assaying to do were drowned. — *Hebrews 11:29.*

Hymn

He knows, and He approves,
The way the righteous go;
But sinners and their works shall meet
A dreadful overthrow.

28. The Giving of the Law

So Moses[1] brought Israel[2] from the Red Sea, and they went out into the wilderness. And the whole congregation murmured against Moses and Aaron[3] and said, "Ye have brought us forth into this wilderness to kill this whole assembly with hunger." Then said the Lord unto Moses, "I have heard the murmurings of the children of Israel. Speak unto them, saying, 'At even ye shall eat flesh, and in the morning ye shall be filled with bread.' "

And at even the quails came up and covered the camp; and in the morning upon the face of the wilderness, there lay a small, round thing. And when the children of Israel saw it, they said, "It is manna." [4] And the children of Israel did eat manna forty years.

In the third month Israel came into the wilderness of Sinai [5] and there camped before the mount. And the Lord said unto Moses, "Go and sanctify [6] the people, and let them wash their clothes and be ready against the third day."

And on the third day in the morning there were thunders and lightnings and a thick cloud upon the mount and the voice of the trumpet exceeding loud, so that all the people trembled. And Moses brought forth the people out of the camp to meet with God; and they stood at the nether[7] part of the mount. And Mount Sinai was altogether on a smoke, because the Lord descended upon it in fire; and the whole mount quaked [8] greatly. And the voice of the trumpet waxed [9] louder and louder. And God spake all these words,[10] even the Ten Commandments.

And all the people removed and stood afar off. And they said unto Moses, "Speak thou with us, and we will hear; but let not God speak with us, lest we die."

And Moses went up into the mount and was in the mount forty days and forty nights.

Explanatory Notes

[1] Mo'-ses. [2] Is'-ra-el. [3] Aa'-ron. [4] See Exodus 16:14-31. [5] Si'-nai. [6] Make holy, prepare. [7] Lower. [8] Trembled. [9] Grew. [10] The Law.

"There were thunders and lightnings and a thick cloud"

Bible Text

There is one Lawgiver, who is able to save and to destroy. — *James 4:12.*

Prayer

Lord, help us to believe in Thee, to love Thee, and to obey Thee in all things; for Jesus' sake. Amen.

29. The Golden Calf

And when the people saw that Moses[1] delayed to come down, they gathered themselves together unto Aaron[2] and said, "Up, make us gods which shall go before us; for as for this Moses, we wot[3] not what is become of him."

And Aaron said, "Break off the golden earrings and bring them unto me." And he received them at their hand and made a molten[4] calf.

And they said, "These be thy gods, O Israel,[5] which brought thee out of Egypt." And they offered burnt offerings and peace offerings. And the people sat down to eat and to drink and rose up to play.[6]

The Lord said to Moses, "Get thee down, thy people have corrupted themselves. It is a stiff-necked[7] people."

And Moses went down from the mount, and two tables[8] were in his hand. And the tables were the work of God, and the writing was the writing of God, graven[9] upon the tables. And as Moses came nigh unto the camp and saw the calf and the dancing, his anger waxed hot; and he cast the tables out of his hands. And he took the calf, and burned it and ground it to powder and strewed it upon the water and made the children of Israel drink of it.

Then Moses stood in the gate of the camp and said, "Who is on the Lord's side? Let him come to me." And all the sons of Levi[10] gathered themselves together unto him. And he said, "Thus saith the Lord, 'Slay every man his brother, his companion, and his neighbor.'" And there fell of the people that day about three thousand men.

And Moses hewed two tables of stone like the first and went up unto Mount Sinai.[11] And the Lord wrote upon the tables the Ten Commandments.

And when Moses came down from the mount, the skin of his face shone while[12] he talked with the Lord.

Explanatory Notes

[1] Mo'-ses. [2] Aa'-ron. [3] Know. [4] Cast from the golden earrings. [5] Is'-ra-el. [6] Like the heathen. [7] Stubborn. [8] Slabs of stone. [9] Carved. [10] Le'-vi. [11] Si'-nai. [12] Because.

"Thy people have corrupted themselves"

Bible Text

Neither be ye idolaters, as were some of them; as it is written, The people sat down to eat and drink and rose up to play. — *1 Corinthians 10:7.*

Prayer

Lord, help us to fear Thee, to love Thee, and to trust in Thee above all things; for Jesus' sake. Amen.

30. The Spies.— The Brazen[1] Serpent

And the children of Israel[2] removed from the desert of Sinai.[3] And the Lord spake unto Moses,[4] saying, "Send thou men that they may search the land of Canaan."[5] And Moses sent them. And they returned after forty days and said, "We came unto the land, and surely it floweth with milk and honey. But we be not able to go up against the people; for they are stronger than we. We were as grasshoppers in their sight."

And all the congregation cried, "Would God that we had died in the land of Egypt[6] or in the wilderness! Let us make a captain and return into Egypt." And Joshua[7] and Caleb,[8] which were of them that searched the land, rent their clothes and said, "The land is an exceeding good land. If the Lord delight in us, then He will bring us into this land; only rebel not ye against the Lord." But all the congregation bade[9] stone them with stones.

And the Lord said, "I have heard the murmurings of the children of Israel against Me. As ye have spoken, so will I do to you. All of you from twenty years old upward, doubtless ye shall not come into the land, save Caleb and Joshua. But your little ones will I bring in. And your children shall wander in the wilderness forty years; and ye shall know My breach of promise."[10]

And the people were much discouraged because of the way, and they spake against God and against Moses. And the Lord sent fiery serpents[11] among the people. And Moses prayed for the people. And the Lord said unto Moses, "Make thee a fiery serpent and set it upon a pole; every one that is bitten, when he looketh upon it, shall live." And Moses made a serpent of brass and put it upon a pole; and if a serpent had bitten any man, when he beheld the serpent of brass, he lived.

Explanatory Notes

[1] Made of brass. [2] Is'-ra-el. [3] Si'-nai. [4] Mo'-ses. [5] Ca'-naan. [6] E'-gypt. [7] Josh'-u-a. [8] Ca'-leb. [9] Urged. [10] What it means when I withdraw my loving-kindness. [11] Very dangerous snakes.

"The land is an exceeding good land"

Bible Text

As Moses lifted up the serpent in the wilderness, even so must the Son of Man be lifted up. — *John 3:14.*

Prayer

Dear Father in heaven, help us to serve Thee on earth and bring us into the glory of heaven; for Jesus' sake. Amen.

31. Israel's[1] Entrance into Canaan[2]

And Moses[3] went up unto the mountain of Nebo.[4] And the Lord showed him all the land and said unto him, "This is the land which I sware unto Abraham,[5] unto Isaac,[6] and unto Jacob,[7] saying, 'I will give it unto thy seed.' I have caused thee to see it, but thou shalt not go over thither."

So Moses, the servant of the Lord, died. And He buried him; but no man knoweth of his sepulcher.[8] And the children of Israel wept for Moses thirty days.

After the death of Moses the Lord spake unto Joshua,[9] saying, "Now, arise, go over this Jordan[10] unto the land which I do give to the children of Israel. Unto this people shalt thou divide the land. Only be thou strong and very courageous. This Book of the Law shall not depart out of thy mouth; but thou shalt meditate[11] therein day and night; for then thou shalt make thy way prosperous[12] and have good success."

Then Joshua commanded the officers of the people, saying, "Prepare you victuals;[13] for within three days ye shall pass over this Jordan."

And when the people removed from their tents, and the priests bearing the Ark of the Covenant[14] before the people were come unto Jordan, and the feet of the priests were dipped in the brim of the water, the waters which came down from above stood and rose up upon an heap very far, and those that came down toward the Salt Sea[15] failed[16] and were cut off. And all the Israelites passed over on dry ground. And when the priests' feet were lifted up unto the dry land, the waters of Jordan returned unto their place and flowed as they did before. And the children of Israel kept the Passover; and they did eat of the old corn of the land. And the manna ceased.[17]

Explanatory Notes

[1] Is'-ra-el. [2] Ca'-naan. [3] Mo'-ses. [4] Ne'-bo. [5] A'-bra-ham.
[6] I'-saac. [7] Ja'-cob. [8] Grave. [9] Josh'-u-a. [10] Jor'-dan. [11] Read it and think upon it. [12] Be successful. [13] Food. [14] See Exodus 25:10-22.
[15] Dead Sea. [16] Ran off. [17] Stopped.

"All the Israelites passed over on dry ground"

Bible Text

Blessed are they that keep His testimonies and that seek Him with the whole heart. — *Psalm 119:2.*

Hymn

Heaven is my fatherland;
Heaven is my home.

32. The Conquest[1] of Canaan[2]

Now, Jericho[3] was straitly[4] shut up because of the children of Israel.[5] And the Lord said unto Joshua,[6] "See, I have given into thine hand Jericho. And ye shall compass[7] the city, all ye men of war, and go round about the city once. Thus shalt thou do six days. And the seventh day ye shall compass the city seven times, and the priests shall blow with trumpets. And all the people shall shout with a great shout; and the wall of the city shall fall down flat."

And so they did. And on the seventh day they compassed the city seven times. And at the seventh time, when the priests blew the trumpets, Joshua said unto the people, "Shout!" So the people shouted; and the wall fell down flat; and they took the city and burned it with fire.

And the five kings of the Amorites[8] gathered themselves together. And the Lord said unto Joshua, "Fear them not, for I have delivered them into thine hand." Joshua therefore came unto them suddenly. And the Lord discomfited [9] them before Israel. And as they fled from before Israel, the Lord cast down great stones from heaven upon them, and they died. They were more which died with hailstones than they whom the children of Israel slew with the sword.

Then spake Joshua to the Lord in the sight of Israel. "Sun, stand thou still!" And the sun stood still and hasted not to go down about a whole day, until the people had avenged themselves[10] upon their enemies.

And the Lord gave unto Israel all the land which He sware to give unto their fathers; and they possessed it and dwelt therein. There failed not aught of any good thing which the Lord had spoken unto the house of Israel; all came to pass.[11]

Explanatory Notes
[1] Capture of all the land. [2] Ca'-naan. [3] Jer'-i-cho. [4] Tightly. [5] Is'-ra-el. [6] Josh'-u-a. [7] Go around. [8] Am'-o-rites. [9] Defeated. [10] Taken revenge. [11] As God's promises are always fulfilled.

"Joshua said unto the people, 'Shout!'"

Bible Text
By faith the walls of Jericho fell down. — *Hebrews 11:30.*

Hymn
A mighty Fortress is our God,
A trusty Shield and Weapon;
He helps us free from every need
That hath us now o'ertaken.

33. Gideon[1]

The children of Israel[2] did evil in the sight of the Lord; and the Lord delivered them into the hand of Midian[3] seven years. And the Midianites[4] destroyed the increase of the earth[5] and left no sustenance[6] for Israel. And the children of Israel cried unto the Lord.

And Gideon threshed wheat by the wine press. And the Angel of the Lord appeared unto him and said, "Go, and thou shalt save Israel from the Midianites." The Spirit of the Lord came upon Gideon, and he blew a trumpet and sent messengers. And Israel gathered after him.

And the Lord said unto Gideon, "The people with thee are too many, lest[7] Israel vaunt[8] themselves, saying, 'Mine own hand hath saved me.' Whosoever is fearful and afraid, let him return." And there returned twenty and two thousand, and there remained ten thousand.

And the Lord said unto Gideon, "The people are yet too many; bring them down unto the water. Every one that lappeth of the water with his tongue as a dog lappeth, him shalt thou set by himself." And the number of them that lapped were three hundred men. And the Lord said, "By the three hundred men will I save you."

And the Midianites lay along in the valley like grasshoppers for multitude.[9] And Gideon divided the three hundred men into three companies, and he put a trumpet in every man's hand, with empty pitchers and lamps[10] within the pitchers. And he said, "Look on me and do likewise. When I blow with the trumpet, then blow ye the trumpets also and say, 'The sword of the Lord and of Gideon.'" And the three companies blew the trumpets and brake the pitchers and held the lamps and cried. And the Lord set every man's sword against his fellow, and the host fled.

Explanatory Notes

[1] Gid'-e-on. [2] Is'-ra-el. [3] Mid'-i-an. [4] Mid'-i-an-ites. [5] Crops.
[6] Things needed to support this life. [7] That not. [8] Boast. [9] Great number. [10] Torches.

"The three companies blew the trumpets"

Bible Text

It is better to trust in the Lord than to put confidence in man. — *Psalm 118:8.*

Hymn

Myself I cannot save,
　　Myself I cannot keep;
But strength in Thee I surely have,
　　Whose eyelids never sleep.

34. Samson[1] — Part One

And the Lord delivered Israel[2] into the hand of the Philistines[3] forty years. And the Angel of the Lord appeared unto the wife of Manoah[4] and said, "Thou shalt bear a son. No razor shall come on his head, for the child shall be a Nazarite;[5] and he shall deliver Israel out of the hands of the Philistines." And the woman bare a son and called his name Samson; and the child grew, and the Lord blessed him; and the Spirit of the Lord began to move him.

And Samson went down to Timnath and saw a woman of the daughters of the Philistines; and he told his father and his mother and said, "Get her for me to wife." But his father and his mother knew not that it was of the Lord, that he sought an occasion[6] against the Philistines. Then went Samson down and his father and his mother to Timnath; and, behold, a young lion roared against him. And the Spirit of the Lord came mightily upon him, and he rent him as he would have rent a kid, and he had nothing in his hand. And after a time, behold, there was a swarm of bees and honey in the carcass of the lion.

And Samson made a feast, and they brought thirty companions to be with him. And Samson said, "I will now put forth a riddle: Out of the eater came forth meat, and out of the strong came forth sweetness." And they could not in three days expound the riddle. And they said unto Samson's wife, "Entice thy husband that he may declare unto us the riddle, lest we burn thee and thy father's house." And Samson's wife wept before him, and on the seventh day he told her. And she told the riddle to her people. And the men of the city said unto him, "What is sweeter than honey? And what is stronger than a lion?"

And the Spirit of the Lord came upon him, and he slew thirty men, and he went up to his father's house.

Explanatory Notes

[1] Sam'-son. [2] Is'-ra-el. [3] Phi-lis'-tines. [4] Ma-no'-ah. [5] Naz'-a-rite, one dedicated to serve God. [6] Chance to punish.

"A young lion roared against him"

Bible Text

He hath said, I will never leave thee nor forsake thee. — *Hebrews 13:5.*

Prayer

Lord, make us obedient to Thee and to our parents, and help us always to do Thy will. Amen.

35. Samson¹ — Part Two

Then the Philistines² went up and pitched in Judah; ³ and the men of Judah said, "Why are ye come up against us?" And they answered, "To bind Samson." And they bound him with two new cords. And the Philistines shouted against him; and the Spirit of the Lord came upon him, and the cords upon his arms became as flax that was burned with fire. And he found a new jawbone of an ass and slew a thousand men therewith.

And it came to pass afterward that he loved Delilah.⁴ And the lords of the Philistines said unto her, "See wherein his great strength lieth. And we will give thee, every one of us, eleven hundred pieces of silver." And when she pressed him daily with her words, he told her, "There hath not a razor come upon my head, for I have been a Nazarite⁵ unto God." And she made him sleep and called for a man; and she caused him to shave off the seven locks of his head. And his strength went from him. And he wist ⁶ not that the Lord was departed from him. But the Philistines took him and put out his eyes and brought him down to Gaza.⁷

Then the lords of the Philistines gathered together to offer a great sacrifice unto Dagon,⁸ their god. And they called for Samson out of the prison house. And he made them sport; ⁹ and they set him between the pillars.¹⁰ Now, the house was full of men and women, and there were upon the roof about three thousand. And Samson called unto the Lord and said, "O Lord God, remember me and strengthen me only this once." And Samson took hold of the two middle pillars, and he bowed himself with all his might; and the house fell upon the lords and upon all the people that were therein; so the dead which he slew at his death were more than they which he slew in his life.

Explanatory Notes

¹ Sam′-son. ² Phi-lis′-tines. ³ Ju′-dah. ⁴ De-li′-lah. ⁵ Naz′-a-rite. ⁶ Knew. ⁷ Ga′-za. ⁸ Da′-gon. ⁹ Entertained them. ¹⁰ Posts on which the house rested.

"*Samson took hold of the two middle pillars*"

Bible Text

Wisdom is better than strength. — *Ecclesiastes 9:16.*

Prayer

Dear father in heaven, bless our homes and grant that all husbands and wives may love and honor each other; for Jesus' sake. Amen.

36. Ruth

There was a famine in the land. And Elimelech[1] and his wife Naomi[2] and his two sons Mahlon[3] and Chilion[4] came into the country of Moab.[5] And Elimelech died, and she was left and her two sons. And they took them wives of the women of Moab. The name of the one was Orpah[6] and the name of the other Ruth. They dwelt there about ten years; and Mahlon and Chilion died.

Then she arose, and her two daughters-in-law, to return unto the land of Judah.[7] And Naomi said, "Go, return each to her mother's house." And Orpah kissed her, but Ruth clave[8] to her. And Ruth said, "Whither thou goest I will go, and where thou lodgest[9] I will lodge; thy people shall be my people and thy God my God."

So they two went until they came to Bethlehem.[10] And Ruth gleaned[11] in the field after the reapers[12] on a part of the field belonging to Boaz,[13] who was of the kindred of Elimelech. And Boaz said unto Ruth, "Go not to glean in another field, but abide here fast[14] by my maidens." And Ruth said unto him, "Why have I found grace in thine eyes?" And Boaz answered, "It hath fully been showed me all that thou hast done unto thy mother-in-law. The Lord recompense thy work, and a full reward be given thee of the Lord God of Israel. And Boaz commanded his young men, "Let her glean even among the sheaves and let fall also some of the handfuls that she may glean them."

And Boaz said unto the elders and unto all the people, "I have bought all that was Elimelech's. Moreover, Ruth, the wife of Mahlon, have I purchased to be my wife." So Boaz took Ruth, and she was his wife. And Boaz begat Obed; and Obed begat Jesse; and Jesse begat David.[15]

Explanatory Notes

[1] E-lim'-e-lech. [2] Na-o'-mi. [3] Mah'-lon. [4] Chil'-i-on. [5] Mo'-ab. [6] Or'-pah. [7] Ju'-dah. [8] Stayed with her. [9] Where you stay. [10] Beth'-le-hem. [11] Gathered grain, as poor people were allowed to do. [12] Grain cutters. [13] Bo'-az. [14] Close. [15] Jesus came from the house of David.

"Ruth gleaned in the field after the reapers"

Bible Text

And there shall come forth a Rod out of the stem of Jesse, and a Branch shall grow out of his roots. — *Isaiah 11:1.*

Prayer

Dear Father in heaven, help us to follow the example of Ruth in obeying our parents; for Jesus' sake. Amen.

37. Samuel [1]

Elkanah[2] had two wives, Hannah[3] and Peninnah.[4] Peninnah had children, but Hannah had no children. And she prayed unto the Lord and said, "O Lord of hosts, if Thou wilt give unto Thine handmaid a man child, then I will give him unto the Lord all the days of his life."

And the Lord remembered Hannah. And she bare a son and called his name Samuel. When she had weaned him, she took him to the house of the Lord to Eli.[5]

Now, the sons of Eli were the sons of Belial.[6] Eli was very old and heard all that his sons did.

And there came a man of God unto Eli and said. "Thus saith the Lord, 'Thou honorest thy sons above Me. Them that honor Me I will honor, and they that despise Me shall be lightly esteemed.[7] Thy two sons, in one day they shall die, both of them.' "

And Samuel was laid down to sleep in the Temple. And the Lord said unto Samuel, "Behold, I will perform against Eli all things which I have spoken concerning his house." And Samuel feared to tell Eli.

Then Eli called Samuel and said, "What is the thing that the Lord hath said unto thee?" And Samuel told him. And he said, "It is the Lord. Let Him do what seemeth Him good."

Now, Israel went out against the Philistines to battle. The two sons of Eli were there with the Ark of the Covenant[8] of God. And Israel was smitten; and the Ark of God was taken, and the two sons of Eli were slain. And there ran a man out of the army to Eli and said, "Israel is fled, and there hath been a great slaughter among the people; and thy two sons are dead; and the Ark of God is taken." And when he made mention of the Ark of God, Eli fell from off the seat backward, and his neck brake, and he died.

Explanatory Notes

[1] Sam'-u-el. [2] El'-ka-nah. [3] Han'-nah. [4] Pe-nin'-nah. [5] E'-li. [6] Be'-li-al; godless men. [7] Thought little of. [8] See Exodus 25:10-22 for a description.

"She took him to the house of the Lord to Eli"

Bible Text

The Lord knoweth the way of the righteous; but the way of the ungodly shall perish. — *Psalm 1:6.*

Prayer

Lord, help us to love Thee and to obey Thee in everything; for Jesus' sake. Amen.

38. Saul

Now, when Samuel[1] was old, all the elders of Israel[2] came to him and said, "Make us a king to judge us like all the nations." But the thing displeased Samuel. And the Lord said unto him, "Hearken unto the voice of the people; for they have not rejected[3] thee, but they have rejected Me, that I should not reign[4] over them."

And when Samuel had caused all the tribes of Israel to come near, Saul, the son of Kish, was taken; [5] and when they sought him, he could not be found. Therefore they inquired of the Lord. And the Lord answered, "Behold, he hath hid himself among the stuff." [6] And they ran and fetched[7] him thence. And when he stood among the people, all the people shouted and said, "God save the king!"

Then the Ammonites[8] came up and encamped against Jabesh.[9] And the Spirit of God came upon Saul. And the fear of the Lord fell on the people; and they came out with one consent and slew the Ammonites.

Samuel also said unto Saul, "Thus saith the Lord of hosts, 'Go and smite Amalek[10] and utterly destroy all that they have and spare them not.' " And Saul smote the Amalekites.[11] But he and the people spared the best of the sheep and of the oxen and all that was good.

And when Samuel came to Saul, Saul said unto him, "I have performed the commandment of the Lord." And Samuel said, "What meaneth, then, this bleating of the sheep and the lowing of the oxen which I hear?" And Saul said, "The people spared the best of the sheep and of the oxen to sacrifice unto the Lord; the rest we have utterly destroyed." Then Samuel said, "Wherefore didst thou not obey the voice of the Lord? Behold, to obey is better than sacrifice.[12] Because thou hast rejected the word of the Lord, He hath also rejected thee from being king."

Explanatory Notes
[1] Sam'-u-el. [2] Is'-ra-el. [3] Cast off. [4] Rule. [5] Was chosen king.
[6] Baggage of the assembly. [7] Brought. [8] Am'-mo-nites. [9] Ja'-besh.
[10] Am'-a-lek. [11] Am'-a-lek-ites. [12] No man dare set God's word aside.

"The Lord hath rejected thee from being king"

Bible Text

Because thou hast rejected knowledge, I will also reject thee. — *Hosea 4:6.*

Hymn

Abide, O dearest Jesus,
Among us with Thy grace
That Satan may not harm us
Nor we to sin give place.

39. The Anointing of David[1]

The Lord said unto Samuel,[2] "Go to Jesse,[3] for I have provided Me a king among his sons." Then Samuel anointed[4] David in the midst of his brethren. And the Spirit of the Lord came upon David; but the Spirit of the Lord departed from Saul, and an evil spirit troubled him And Saul sent unto Jesse and said, "Send me David, thy son." And David came to Saul. And when the evil spirit was upon Saul, David took an harp and played; so Saul was refreshed, and the evil spirit departed.

Now, the Philistines[5] gathered together their armies to battle. And there went out a champion out of the camp of the Philistines named Goliath,[6] whose height was six cubits and a span.[7] And the weight of his coat of mail[8] was five thousand shekels[9] of brass, and the staff of his spear was like a weaver's beam.[10]

And he stood and cried unto the armies of Israel, "Choose you a man for you and let him come down to me. If he be able to kill me, then will we be your servants; but if I kill him, then shall ye be our servants." When Saul and all Israel heard these words, they were greatly afraid. And the Philistine drew near morning and evening and presented himself forty days.

Then David returned to feed his father's sheep at Bethlehem. And Jesse said unto David, "Run to the camp and look how thy brethren fare." And David came and saluted his brethren. And, behold, there came up the champion and spake the same words. And David said, "Who is this uncircumcised[11] Philistine that he should defy[12] the armies of the living God?" And they rehearsed[13] David's words before Saul: and he sent for him.

Explanatory Notes

[1] Da'-vid. [2] Sam'-u-el. [3] Jes'-se. [4] Poured a sweet-smelling oil over him. [5] Phi-lis'-tines. [6] Go-li'-ath. [7] Cubit, 1½ ft.; span, 9 in.; whole height of Goliath, 9 ft. 9 in. [8] Armor. [9] About 150 pounds. [10] A round beam, 4 or 5 inches in diameter. [11] Heathen. [12] Speak against. [13] Repeated.

"Then Samuel anointed David"

Bible Text

There is no power but of God; the powers that be are ordained of God. — *Romans 13:1.*

Prayer

O God, Thou Ruler of heaven and earth, give those who govern our country the wisdom to seek Thy will. Amen.

40. David[1] and Goliath[2]

And David said to Saul, "Thy servant will go and fight with this Philistine." [3]

And Saul said, "Thou art not able to go against this Philistine to fight with him; for thou art but a youth, and he a man of war from his youth."

David said, "The Lord will deliver me out of the hand of this Philistine."

And Saul said unto David, "Go, and the Lord be with thee." And Saul armed David with his armor, and he put a helmet of brass upon his head; also he armed him with a coat of mail.

And David assayed[4] to go; and he said unto Saul, "I cannot go with these; for I have not proved them." [5] And David put them off him. And he took his staff and five smooth stones out of the brook, and his sling was in his hand; and he drew near to the Philistine.

And when the Philistine saw David, he said, "Am I a dog that thou comest to me with staves?" [6]

Then said David, "Thou comest to me with a sword and with a spear and with a shield; but I come to thee in the name of the Lord of Hosts.[7] This day will the Lord deliver thee into mine hand, that all the earth may know that there is a God in Israel." [8]

And David took a stone and slang it and smote the Philistine, that the stone sunk into his forehead; and he fell upon his face to the earth. And David ran and stood upon the Philistine; and he took his sword and cut off his head therewith. And when the Philistines saw that their champion was dead, they fled. And the men of Israel and Judah[9] pursued them; and the wounded of the Philistines fell down by the way.

Explanatory Notes

[1] Da'-vid. [2] Go-li'-ath. [3] Phi-lis'-tine. [4] Tried. [5] Am not used to them. [6] Sticks. [7] The Lord of many. [8] Is'-ra-el. [9] Ju'-dah.

"And David took a stone and slang it"

Bible Text
The Lord taketh pleasure in them that fear Him, in those that hope in His mercy. — *Psalm 147:11.*

Prayer
Lord, help us always to remember that as long as we trust in Thee, we shall be strong. Amen.

41. David's Fall and Repentance

And David[1] sent Joab[2] and his servants with him; and they destroyed the children of Ammon[3] and besieged Rabbah.[4] But David tarried[5] still at Jerusalem.[6]

And in an eveningtide[7] David walked upon the roof of the king's house; and he saw Bathsheba,[8] the wife of Uriah,[9] washing herself. And David sent messengers and took her and lay with her.

And David wrote a letter to Joab. And he wrote, "Set ye Uriah in the forefront of the hottest battle and retire ye from him that he may be smitten and die."

And when the wife of Uriah heard that her husband was dead, she mourned for him. And when the mourning was past, David sent and fetched her to his house; and she became his wife and bare him a son.

But the thing displeased the Lord, and the Lord sent Nathan[10] unto David. And he said unto him, "There were two men in one city, the one rich and the other poor. The rich man had exceeding many flocks and herds; but the poor man had nothing save one little ewe lamb. And there came a traveler unto the rich man, and he spared to take of his own flock, but took the poor man's lamb."

And David's anger was greatly kindled,[11] and he said, "As the Lord liveth, the man that hath done this thing shall surely die." And Nathan said to David, "Thou art the man! Thou hast slain Uriah with the sword of the children of Ammon and hast taken his wife." And David said unto Nathan, "I have sinned against the Lord." And Nathan said unto David, "The Lord hath also put away thy sin; thou shalt not die. Howbeit,[12] because by this deed thou hast given great occasion to the enemies of the Lord to blaspheme,[13] the child that is born unto thee shall surely die."

Explanatory Notes

[1] Da'-vid. [2] Jo'-ab. [3] Am'-mon. [4] Rab'-bah. [5] Stayed. [6] Je-ru'-sa-lem. [7] Evening. [8] Bath-she'-ba. [9] U-ri'-ah. [10] Na'-than. [11] Stirred up. [12] But. [13] To talk evil, to mock.

"I have sinned against the Lord"

Bible Text

Have mercy upon me, O God, according to Thy loving-kindness; according unto the multitude of Thy tender mercies blot out my transgressions. — *Psalm 51:1.*

Prayer

Create in me a clean heart, O God; and renew a right spirit within me; for Jesus' sake. Amen.

42. Absalom's [1] Rebellion

In all Israel[2] there was none to be so much praised for his beauty as Absalom, the son of David; [3] from the sole of his foot even to the crown of his head there was no blemish[4] in him. And Absalom said, "Oh, that I were made judge in the land!" And when any man came to do him obeisance,[5] he put forth his hand and took him and kissed him. So Absalom stole the hearts of the men of Israel.

And Absalom said unto the king, "Let me go and pay my vow[6] which I have vowed unto the Lord in Hebron." [7] And the king said unto him, "Go in peace." So he went to Hebron. But Absalom sent spies throughout all the tribes of Israel, saying, "As soon as ye hear the sound of the trumpet, then ye shall say, 'Absalom reigneth in Hebron.' " And the people increased continually with Absalom.[8]

And a messenger told David. And David said unto all his servants, "Arise, and let us flee from Absalom."

And Absalom and the men of Israel came to Jerusalem.[9] Then David arose and all the people that were with him, and they passed over Jordan.[10] And Absalom also passed over Jordan, he and all the men of Israel with him. And the king commanded the captains, saying, "Deal gently with the young man, even with Absalom."

And the people of Israel were slain before the servants of David.[11] And Absalom rode upon a mule; and the mule went under the thick boughs of a great oak, and his head caught hold of the oak, and he was taken up[12] between the heaven and the earth; and the mule that was under him went away. Then Joab took three darts[13] and thrust them through the heart of Absalom. And they took Absalom and cast him into a great pit and laid a very great heap of stones upon him.

Explanatory Notes

[1] Ab'-sa-lom.   [2] Is'-ra-el.   [3] Da'-vid.   [4] Bodily fault.   [5] To bow in honor.   [6] Fulfill my promise.   [7] He'-bron.   [8] Flocked to the rebel. [9] Je-ru'-sa-lem.   [10] Jor'-dan.   [11] Absalom's army was defeated. [12] Caught.   [13] Spears.

"The mule went under the thick boughs of a great oak"

Bible Text

He that wasteth his father and chaseth away his mother is a son that causeth shame and bringeth reproach. — *Proverbs 19:26.*

Prayer

O God, save us from unbelief and disobedience, and make us glad to serve Thee and our parents; for Jesus' sake. Amen.

43. King Solomon[1] and the Temple

Solomon sat upon the throne of David.[2] And Solomon loved the Lord. And the Lord appeared to Solomon in a dream. God said, "Ask what I shall give thee."

And Solomon said, "O Lord, I am but a little child; I know not how to go out or come in. Give therefore Thy servant an understanding heart to judge Thy people that I may discern[3] between good and bad."

And the speech pleased the Lord, and God said to him, "Behold, I have given thee a wise and an understanding heart; and I have also given thee that which thou hast not asked, both riches and honor. And if thou wilt walk in My ways, then I will lengthen thy days."[4]

Then Solomon began to build the house of the Lord at Jerusalem.[5] He was seven years in building the house.

And all the men of Israel[6] assembled themselves unto King Solomon; and the priests brought in the Ark of the Covenant of the Lord to the Most Holy Place. And when the priests were come out of the Holy Place, the glory of the Lord filled the house of the Lord.

And Solomon stood before the altar and spread forth his hands toward heaven and said, "Lord God of Israel, behold, the heaven and heaven of heavens cannot contain[7] Thee; how much less this house! Yet have thou respect unto the prayer of Thy servant that Thine eyes may be open toward this house night and day. When Thy people Israel be smitten down before the enemy; if there be in the land famine;[8] if there be pestilence,[9] whatsoever plague[10] or sickness there be, and they make supplication[11] unto Thee in this house, then hear Thou their prayer and forgive Thy people that have sinned against Thee."

Explanatory Notes

[1] Sol'-o-mon. [2] Da'-vid. [3] See clearly. [4] Give you a long life.
[5] Je-ru'-sa-lem. [6] Is'-ra-el. [7] Are not large enough to hold Thee.
[8] General scarcity of food. [9] Widespread sickness. [10] Trouble.
[11] Humble prayer.

"And Solomon stood before the altar"

Bible Text

If any of you lack wisdom, let him ask of God, and it shall be given him. — *James 1:5.*

Prayer

Dear Father in heaven, let us never forget to call upon Thee in every trouble, and to come before Thee with prayer, praise, and thanksgiving; for Jesus' sake. Amen.

44. The Prophet Elijah[1]

Ahab[2] was king of Israel.[3] And he served Baal[4] and did more to provoke God to anger than all the kings of Israel before him. And Elijah the prophet said unto Ahab, "As the Lord God of Israel liveth, there shall not be dew nor rain these years but according to my word."

And the word of the Lord came unto him saying, "Hide thyself by the brook Cherith;[5] I have commanded the ravens to feed thee there." So he did according unto the word of the Lord. And the ravens brought him bread and flesh in the morning and in the evening.

And the brook dried up because there had been no rain in the land. And the word of the Lord came unto Elijah, saying, "Get thee to Zarephath;[6] I have commanded a widow woman there to sustain[7] thee."

So he went. And the widow was gathering sticks; and he called to her and said, "Fetch me a little water that I may drink." And as she was going, he called to her and said, "Bring me a morsel[8] of bread in thine hand."

And she said, "I have not a cake, but an handful of meal in a barrel and a little oil in a cruse." [9]

Elijah said unto her, "Fear not; for thus saith the Lord, 'The barrel of meal shall not waste,[10] neither shall the cruse of oil fail, until the day that the Lord sendeth rain upon the earth.' " And she and he and her house did eat many days. The barrel of meal wasted not, neither did the cruse of oil fail, according to the word of the Lord.

After these things the son of the woman fell sick that there was no breath left in him. And Elijah said unto her. "Give me thy son." And he cried unto the Lord. And the Lord heard the voice of Elijah; and the soul of the child came into him again, and he revived.[11]

Explanatory Notes

[1] E-li'-jah. [2] A'-hab. [3] Is'-ra-el. [4] Ba'-al, a false god. [5] Che'-rith. [6] Zar'-e-phath. [7] Support. [8] A bit. [9] A vessel. [10] Be used up. [11] Came to life.

"The ravens brought him bread and flesh"

Bible Text

Behold, the eye of the Lord is upon them that fear Him, upon them that hope in His mercy, to deliver their soul from death and to keep them alive in famine. — *Psalm 33:18-19.*

Prayer

Lord, help us to trust in Thee and to believe that Thou wilt richly and daily provide us with all that we need for our support. Amen.

45. Elijah[1] and the Prophets of Baal[2]

Elijah came unto all the people and said, "How long halt[3] ye between two opinions? If the Lord be God, follow Him; but if Baal, then follow him." And the people answered him not a word. Then said Elijah unto the people, "Give us two bullocks;[4] and let the prophets of Baal choose one bullock and lay it on wood and put no fire under, and I will dress the other bullock and lay it on wood and put no fire under. Ye call on the name of your gods, and I will call on the name of the Lord. The God that answereth by fire, let Him be God."

And all the people answered, "It is well spoken."

And the prophets of Baal took the bullock; and they dressed it and called from morning even until noon, "O Baal, hear us!" But there was no voice nor any that answered.

And Elijah said unto all the people, "Come near unto me." And he built an altar, and made a trench[5] about the altar, and laid the bullock on the wood, and said, "Pour water on the burnt sacrifice." And the water ran about the altar; and he filled the trench also with water. And Elijah said, "Lord God of Abraham,[6] Isaac,[7] and of Israel,[8] let it be known this day that Thou art God in Israel, and that I am Thy servant. Hear me, O Lord; hear me!"

Then the fire of the Lord fell and consumed[9] the burnt sacrifice and the wood and the stones and the dust and licked up the water that was in the trench.

And when all the people saw it, they fell on their faces and said, "The Lord, He is the God! The Lord, He is the God!"

And Elijah said unto them, "Take the prophets of Baal." And they took them. And Elijah brought them down to the brook Kishon[10] and slew them there.

Explanatory Notes

[1] E-li'-jah. [2] Ba'-al. [3] Waver. [4] Young bulls. [5] Ditch. [6] A'-bra-ham. [7] I'-saac. [8] Is'-ra-el. [9] Burned it up completely. [10] Ki'-shon.

"The Lord, He is the God!"

Bible Text

Thou shalt worship the Lord, thy God, and Him only shalt thou serve. — *Matthew 4:10.*

Hymn

Holy Spirit, all divine,
Dwell within this heart of mine;
Cast down every idol-throne,
Reign supreme, and reign alone.

46. Naboth's[1] Vineyard

Naboth had a vineyard hard[2] by the palace of Ahab,[3] king of Samaria.[4] And Ahab spake unto Naboth, saying, "Give me thy vineyard because it is near unto my house, and I will give thee for it a better vineyard than it or the worth of it in money."

And Naboth said, "The Lord forbid it me that I should give the inheritance of my fathers unto thee."

And Ahab came into his house heavy[5] and displeased. And he laid him down upon his bed and would eat no bread. But Jezebel,[6] his wife, came to him and said, "Arise and eat bread and let thine heart be merry; I will give thee the vineyard of Naboth."

So she wrote letters in Ahab's name and sent them unto the elders and nobles, saying, "Proclaim a fast[7] and set Naboth on high among the people;[8] and set two men before him to bear witness against him, saying, 'Thou didst blaspheme[9] God and the king'; and then carry him out and stone him." [10]   And the men did as Jezebel had sent unto them.

And Jezebel said to Ahab, "Arise, take possession of the vineyard of Naboth, for Naboth is dead."

And the word of the Lord came to Elijah,[11] saying, "Arise, go down to meet Ahab; behold, he is in the vineyard of Naboth, whither he is gone down to possess it.[12] And thou shalt speak to him, saying, 'Thus saith the Lord, "Hast thou killed and also taken possession? In the place where dogs licked the blood of Naboth shall dogs lick thy blood. The dogs shall eat Jezebel by the walls of Jezreel.[13] Him that dieth of Ahab in the city the dogs shall eat, and him that dieth in the field shall the fowls of the air eat." ' "

And it came to pass according to the word of the Lord.

Explanatory Notes

[1] Na'-both. [2] Close. [3] A'-hab. [4] Sa-ma'-ri-a. [5] Angry. [6] Jez'-e-bel. [7] As a sign that something terrible had happened. [8] As the accused person. [9] Curse. [10] Blaspheming was punished by death. [11] E-li'-jah. [12] Take it. [13] Jez'-re-el.

*"The Lord forbid it me that I should give the inheritance of my fathers
unto thee"*

Bible Text

Thou shalt not covet thy neighbor's house. — *Exodus 20:17.*

Prayer

Lord, help us to fear and love Thee, and let us not seek to get
our neighbor's property unjustly. Hear us for Jesus' sake. Amen.

47. Elijah's[1] Ascension.[2] — Elisha[3]

And it came to pass, when the Lord would take up Elijah into heaven by a whirlwind, that Elijah went with Elisha. And Elijah took his mantle and wrapped it together and smote the water; and they were divided hither and thither, so that they two went over on dry ground.

And it came to pass, when they were gone over, that Elijah said unto Elisha, "Ask what I shall do for thee before I be taken away from thee."

And Elisha said, "I pray thee, let a double portion of thy spirit be upon me."[4]

And it came to pass, as they still went on and talked, that, behold, there appeared a chariot[5] of fire and horses of fire; and Elijah went up by a whirlwind into heaven. And Elisha saw it, and he cried, "My father, my father, the chariot of Israel[6] and the horsemen thereof!" And he saw him no more.

And he took up the mantle of Elijah that fell from him and went back and stood by the bank of Jordan;[7] and he took the mantle of Elijah and smote the waters and said, "Where is the Lord God of Elijah?" And the waters parted hither and thither, and Elisha went over.

And the sons of the prophets which were at Jericho[8] said, "The spirit of Elijah doth rest upon Elisha."

And the men of the city said unto Elisha, "Behold, the situation of this city is pleasant, but the water is naught,[9] and the ground barren."[10]

And he said, "Bring me a new cruse,[11] and put salt therein." And he went forth unto the spring[12] of the waters, and cast the salt in, and said, "Thus saith the Lord, 'I have healed these waters.'" So the waters were healed.

Explanatory Notes

[1] E-li'-jah. [2] Going up into heaven. [3] E-li'-sha. [4] Elisha desired the power of Elijah to do the Lord's work in the best possible way. [5] Two-wheeled wagon. [6] Is'-ra-el. [7] Jor'-dan. [8] Jer'-i-cho. [9] Bad, poisonous. [10] Unfruitful. [11] Bowl. [12] Source.

48. Naaman[1] and Elisha[2]

Naaman, captain of the host of the king of Syria,[3] was a great man; but he was a leper. And the Syrians had brought away captive out of Israel[4] a little maid; and she waited on Naaman's wife. And she said unto her mistress, "Would God my lord were with the prophet in Samaria![5] He would recover[6] him of his leprosy."

And he departed and took with him ten talents of silver[7] and six thousand pieces of gold[8] and ten changes of raiment. So he came with his chariot and stood at the door of the house of Elisha. And Elisha sent a messenger unto him, saying, "Go and wash in Jordan[9] seven times, and thou shalt be clean." But Naaman was wroth and said, "Are not the rivers of Damascus[10] better than all the waters of Israel?" And his servants said, "My father, if the prophet had bid thee do some great thing, wouldst thou not have done it?" Then he went down and dipped himself seven times in Jordan, and he was clean.

And he returned to the man of God and said, "Now I know that there is no God in all the earth but in Israel. Now, therefore, I pray thee, take a blessing[11] of thy servant." And he urged him to take it, but he refused.

But Gehazi[12] followed after Naaman and said, "My master hath sent me, saying, 'Behold, even now there be come to me two young men of the sons of the prophets; give them a talent of silver[13] and two changes of garments.'" Naaman said, "Take two talents." And he urged him.

And Elisha said unto Gehazi, "Whence comest thou?" And he said, "Thy servant went nowhither."[14] And he said unto him, "Is it a time to receive money, and to receive garments? The leprosy, therefore, of Naaman shall cleave unto thee and unto thy seed forever." And he went out from his presence a leper as white as snow.

Explanatory Notes

[1] Na'-a-man. [2] E-li'-sha. [3] Syr'-i-a. [4] Is'-ra-el. [5] Sa-ma'-ri-a. [6] Cure. [7] About $20,000. [8] About $60,000. [9] Jor'-dan. [10] Da-mas'-cus. [11] Present. [12] Ge-ha'-zi. [13] About $2,000. [14] Nowhere.

"Elijah went up by a whirlwind into heaven"

Bible Text

I have fought a good fight, I have finished my course, I have kept the faith; henceforth there is laid up for me a crown of righteousness. — *2 Timothy 4:7-8.*

Hymn

Draw us to Thee, Lord, lovingly;
Let us depart with gladness
That we may be forever free
From sorrow, grief, and sadness.

"Would God my lord were with the prophet in Samaria!"

Bible Text

Thou shalt not steal. — *Exodus 20:15.*

Prayer

Dear Father in heaven, make us honest and true in all things. Help us to serve Thee and not ourselves. Amen.

49. The Three Men in the Fiery Furnace

Nebuchadnezzar,[1] the king of Babylon,[2] made an image[3] of gold and sent to gather all the rulers of the provinces[4] to come to the dedication of the image. Then a herald cried aloud, "O people, at what time ye hear the sound of the cornet, ye shall fall down and worship the golden image! And whoso falleth not down shall be cast into the midst of a burning fiery furnace!" Therefore, when they heard the sound of the cornet, all the people fell down and worshiped the golden image.

At that time certain Chaldeans[5] came near and accused the Jews. They spake, "O king, Shadrach,[6] Meshach,[7] and Abednego[8] worship not the golden image."

Then Nebuchadnezzar said, "If ye worship not the image, ye shall be cast into the furnace; and who is that God that shall deliver you out of my hands?"

They answered and said, "Our God is able to deliver us, and He will deliver us. But if not, be it known unto thee that we will not worship the golden image."

Then was Nebuchadnezzar full of fury and commanded that they should heat the furnace seven times more. Then these men were bound and cast into the fiery furnace.

Then Nebuchadnezzar, the king, was astonished and said, "Did we not cast three men bound into the midst of the fire? Lo, I see four men loose, walking in the midst of the fire, and they have no hurt; and the form of the fourth is like the Son of God." Then Nebuchadnezzar came near the mouth of the burning fiery furnace and said, "Ye servants of the most high God, come forth!" And not an hair of their head was singed.

Then Nebuchadnezzar said, "Blessed be the God of Shadrach, Meshach, and Abednego, who hath sent His angel and delivered His servants that trusted in Him."

Explanatory Notes

[1] Neb-u-chad-nez'-zar. [2] Bab'-y-lon. [3] Statue. [4] States. [5] Chal-de'-ans. [6] Sha'-drach. [7] Me'-shach. [8] A-bed'-ne-go.

"Ye servants of the most high God, come forth!"

Bible Text

Fear not them which kill the body, but are not able to kill the soul; but rather fear Him which is able to destroy both soul and body in hell. — *Matthew 10:28.*

Prayer

Dear God, be with us in danger and keep us faithful when wicked people tempt us; for Jesus' sake. Amen.

50. Daniel[1] in the Lions' Den

And King Darius[2] set over the whole realm[3] three presidents, of whom Daniel was first. Then the presidents and princes sought to find occasion against Daniel; but they could find no fault, forasmuch as he was faithful. Then said these men, "We shall not find any occasion against this Daniel except concerning the Law of his God."

Then these princes assembled together to the king and said, "King Darius, all the presidents and the princes have consulted together to establish a royal statute[4] that whosoever shall ask a petition of any god or man for thirty days save of thee, O king, he shall be cast into the den of lions." Wherefore King Darius signed the decree.[5]

Now, Daniel kneeled three times a day and prayed as he did aforetime. Then these men spake before the king and said, "Daniel regardeth not thee, O king." Then the king was sore displeased with himself and commanded, and they brought Daniel and cast him into the den of lions.

And the king arose very early in the morning and went in haste unto the den of lions; and he cried with a lamentable[6] voice, "O Daniel, servant of the living God, is thy God able to deliver thee from the lions?"

Then said Daniel unto the king, "My God hath sent His angel and hath shut the lions' mouths that they have not hurt me."

Then was the king exceeding glad for him and commanded that they should take Daniel up out of the den.

And the king commanded, and they brought those men which had accused Daniel, and they cast them into the den of lions. Then Darius wrote unto all people, "I make a decree that in every dominion[7] of my kingdom men tremble and fear before the God of Daniel; for He is the living God."

Explanatory Notes

[1] Dan'-iel. [2] Da-ri'-us. [3] Kingdom. [4] Law of the king. [5] Royal order. [6] Sad, weeping. [7] State or province.

"God hath sent His angel and shut the lions' mouths"

Bible Text

Fear thou not, for I am with thee; be not dismayed, for I am thy God. I will strengthen thee; yea, I will uphold thee with the right hand of My righteousness. — *Isaiah 41:10.*

Prayer

Dear God, protect us against the spite of wicked people. Whatever the danger, keep us faithful that we may not forsake Thee; for Jesus' sake. Amen.

The New Testament

1. Zacharias[1]

There was in the days of King Herod[2] a certain priest named Zacharias, and his wife was Elisabeth.[3] They were both righteous before God.[4] And they had no child, and both were now well stricken in years.[5]

And it came to pass that it was Zacharias' lot[6] to burn incense[7] when he went into the Temple of the Lord. And the whole multitude of the people were praying without at the time of incense. And there appeared unto him an angel of the Lord, standing at the right side of the altar of incense. And when Zacharias saw him, he was troubled.[8]

But the angel said unto him, "Fear not, Zacharias, for thy prayer is heard, and thy wife Elisabeth shall bear thee a son, and thou shalt call his name John. He shall be great in the sight of the Lord and shall be filled with the Holy Ghost. And he shall go before Him in the spirit and power of Elias[9] to make ready a people prepared for the Lord." [10]

And Zacharias said unto the angel, "Whereby shall I know this?"

The angel answered, I am Gabriel,[11] that stand in the presence of God, and I am sent to show thee these glad tidings.[12] And, behold, thou shalt be dumb and not able to speak until the day that these things shall be performed,[13] because thou believest not my words."

And the people waited for Zacharias and marveled[14] that he tarried[15] so long in the Temple. And when he came out, he could not speak unto them; and he beckoned[16] unto them and remained speechless.

Explanatory Notes

[1] Zach-a-ri'-as. [2] Her'-od. [3] E-lis'-a-beth. [4] God-fearing. [5] Quite old. [6] Time or turn. [7] Made from the sap of trees; prescribed for offering, Exodus 30:34-36, and of an agreeable odor when burned. [8] Frightened. [9] E-li'-as. [10] He was to prepare the people for the coming of the Savior by telling them about Him. He is often called the forerunner of Christ. [11] Ga'-bri-el. [12] News. [13] Shall happen. [14] Wondered. [15] Stayed. [16] Waved his hand.

"Fear not, Zacharias"

Bible Text

Behold, I will send My messenger, and he shall prepare the way before Me. — *Malachi 3:1.*

Hymn

Lift up your heads, ye mighty gates!
Behold, the King of Glory waits;
The King of Kings is drawing near;
The Savior of the world is here.

2. Announcement to Mary [1]

In the sixth month [2] the angel Gabriel [3] was sent from God unto a city named Nazareth, [4] to a virgin [5] espoused [6] to a man whose name was Joseph, [7] of the house of David; [8] and the virgin's name was Mary. And the angel came in unto her and said, "Hail, [9] thou that art highly favored! [10] The Lord is with thee; blessed art thou among women."

And when she saw him, she was troubled and cast in her mind [11] what manner of salutation [12] this should be.

And the angel said unto her: "Fear not, Mary; for thou hast found favor with God. And, behold, thou shalt bring forth a son and shalt call His name JESUS. [13] He shall be great and shall be called the Son of the Highest. And He shall reign [14] over the house of Jacob forever."

Then said Mary unto the angel, "How shall this be, seeing I know not a man?" [15]

The angel answered and said unto her, "The Holy Ghost shall come upon thee, and the power of the Highest shall overshadow thee; therefore also that Holy Thing which shall be born of thee shall be called the Son of God. For with God nothing shall be impossible."

And Mary said, "Behold the handmaid [16] of the Lord; be it unto me according to thy word." And the angel departed from her.

Behold, the angel of the Lord appeared unto Joseph in a dream, saying, "Joseph, thou son of David, fear not to take unto thee Mary, thy wife. She shall bring forth a Son, and thou shalt call His name JESUS; for He shall save His people from their sins."

Then Joseph did as the angel of the Lord had told him and took unto him his wife.

Explanatory Notes

[1] Ma'-ry. [2] Six months after he had appeared to Zacharias. [3] Ga'-bri-el. [4] Naz'-a-reth. [5] Unmarried woman. [6] Engaged to be married. [7] Jo'-seph. [8] Da'-vid. [9] I greet thee. [10] Honored. [11] Thought about. [12] Greeting. [13] Je'-sus. [14] Rule. [15] I am not yet married. [16] Servant.

"Hail, thou that art highly favored!"

Bible Text

Behold, a virgin shall conceive and bear a Son and shall call His name Immanuel. — *Isaiah 7:14.*

Hymn

Hark the glad sound! The Savior comes,
  The Savior promised long;
Let every heart prepare a throne
  And every voice a song.

115

3. The Birth of John the Baptist

Now, Elisabeth[1] brought forth a son. And her neighbors and cousins[2] heard how the Lord had showed great mercy upon her; and they rejoiced with her.

And on the eighth day they came to circumcise[3] the child; and they called him Zacharias,[4] after the name of his father. And his mother answered and said, "Not so; but he shall be called John."

They said unto her, "There is none of thy kindred[5] that is called by this name." And they made signs to his father how he would have him called.

And he asked for a writing table[6] and wrote, saying, "His name is John."

And they marveled all.

And his mouth was opened immediately and his tongue loosed,[7] and he spake and praised God. And all they that heard this laid it up in their hearts,[8] saying, "What manner of child shall this be!" And the hand of the Lord was with him.

And his father Zacharias was filled with the Holy Ghost and prophesied,[9] saying: "Blessed be the Lord God of Israel;[10] for He hath visited and redeemed His people.[11] And thou, child, shalt be called the prophet of the Highest; for thou shalt go before the face of the Lord[12] to prepare His ways, to give knowledge of salvation[13] unto His people by the remission[14] of their sins.

The child grew and waxed[15] strong in spirit and was in the deserts till the day of his showing unto Israel.

Explanatory Notes

[1] E-lis'-a-beth. [2] Relatives. [3] According to God's command; see Genesis 17:10-14. [4] Zach-a-ri'-as. [5] Family or relatives. [6] Small board covered with wax, used for writing. [7] He was able to speak again. [8] Thought about it. [9] Foretold what would happen. [10] Is'-ra-el. [11] Through Jesus, the Savior. [12] Before Jesus. [13] Tell them how to be saved. [14] Forgiveness. [15] Became.

"His name is John"

Bible Text

The Word of the Lord is right. — *Psalm 33:4.*

Hymn

Redeemer, come! I open wide
My heart to Thee; here, Lord, abide!

117

4. The Birth of Jesus Christ[1]

And it came to pass in those days that there went out a decree[2] from Caesar Augustus[3] that all the world[4] should be taxed.[5] And this taxing was first made when Cyrenius[6] was governor of Syria.[7] And all went to be taxed, every one into his own city.[8]

And Joseph[9] also went up from Galilee,[10] out of the city of Nazareth,[11] into Judea,[12] unto the city of David,[13] which is called Bethlehem,[14] because he was of the house and lineage[15] of David, to be taxed with Mary, his espoused[16] wife, being great with child.

And so it was, that while they were there, the days were accomplished[17] that she should be delivered. And she brought forth her first-born Son and wrapped Him in swaddling clothes[18] and laid Him in a manger,[19] because there was no room for them in the inn.[20]

Explanatory Notes

[1] The coming of the Savior had been foretold thousands of years before His birth. The Prophets in the Old Testament had prophesied the time of His coming and had said that His mother would be a virgin. One of them had even foretold that He would be born in the little town of Bethlehem. These prophecies were now being fulfilled. [2] A law. [3] Cae'-sar Au-gus'-tus — the great Roman emperor. The Holy Land had also become part of his empire. [4] All who belonged to the Roman world empire. [5] Registered for taxation. [6] Cy-re'-ni-us. [7] Syr'-i-a. [8] The city of his ancestors, where the family records were kept. [9] Jo'-seph. [10] Gal'-i-lee [11] Naz'-a-reth. [12] Ju-de'-a. [13] Da'-vid. [14] Beth'-le-hem. [15] Family. [16] To whom he was engaged to be married. [17] The time had come for Jesus to be born. [18] Strips of cloth wrapped around the child, as the custom was in those days. [19] Trough, or box, from which the cattle ate. [20] Lodging place, or hotel, for people who were away from home.

Glory to God in highest heaven,
Who unto us His Son hath given!

"And laid Him in a manger"

Bible Text

Unto us a Child is born; unto us a Son is given. — *Isaiah 9:6.*

Hymn

Ah, dearest Jesus, holy Child,
Make Thee a bed, soft, undefiled,
Within my heart, that it may be
A quiet chamber kept for Thee.

119

5. The Announcement of the Savior's Birth

And there were in the same country shepherds abiding[1] in the field, keeping watch over their flock[2] by night. And, lo, the angel of the Lord came upon them, and the glory of the Lord shone round about them; and they were sore[3] afraid.

And the angel said unto them, "Fear not; for, behold, I bring you good tidings[4] of great joy, which shall be to all people. For unto you is born this day, in the city of David,[5] a Savior, which is Christ[6] the Lord.[7] And this shall be a sign unto you: ye shall find the Babe wrapped in swaddling clothes, lying in a manger."

And suddenly there was with the angel a multitude of the heavenly host,[8] praising God and saying, "Glory to God in the highest, and on earth peace, good will toward men."

And it came to pass, as the angels were gone away from them into heaven, the shepherds said one to another, "Let us now go even unto Bethlehem[9] and see this thing which is come to pass, which the Lord hath made known unto us." And they came with haste[10] and found Mary and Joseph, and the Babe lying in a manger.

And when they had seen it, they made known abroad[11] the saying which was told them concerning this Child. And all they that heard it wondered at those things which were told them by the shepherds.

But Mary kept all these things and pondered[12] them in her heart.

Explanatory Notes

[1] Staying. [2] A flock of sheep. [3] The shepherds were very much afraid when they saw the glory of the Lord, which was brighter than the brightest day. [4] News. [5] Da'-vid. [6] The Anointed, the Messiah. [7] God Himself, Jehovah. [8] A great number of angels. [9] Beth'-le-hem. [10] In a great hurry. [11] Told others whom they met on the way. [12] Thought about.

"Behold, I bring you good tidings of great joy"

Bible Text

God so loved the world that He gave His only-begotten Son, that whosoever believeth in Him should not perish but have everlasting life. — *John 3:16.*

Hymn

Joy to the world, the Lord is come!
Let earth receive her King;
Let every heart prepare Him room
And heaven and nature sing.

6. The Circumcision and the Presentation

And when eight days were accomplished[1] for the circumcising[2] of the Child, His name was called JESUS,[3] which was so named of the angel before He was conceived.

And when the days of her purification[4] according to the Law of Moses[5] were accomplished, they brought Him to Jerusalem[6] to present Him to the Lord[7] and to offer a sacrifice.[8]

And, behold, there was a man in Jerusalem whose name was Simeon;[9] and the same man was just and devout,[10] waiting for the Consolation[11] of Israel;[12] and the Holy Ghost was upon him. And it was revealed[13] unto him by the Holy Ghost that he should not see death before he had seen the Lord's Christ. And he came by the Spirit into the Temple.

And when the parents brought in the Child Jesus, he took Him up in his arms and blessed God and said, "Lord, now lettest Thou Thy servant depart in peace[14] according to Thy word; for mine eyes have seen Thy salvation, which Thou hast prepared before the face of all people; a light to lighten the Gentiles[15] and the glory of Thy people Israel.

And Joseph and His mother marveled at those things which were spoken of Him.

And there was one Anna, a prophetess. She was a widow of about fourscore and four years, which departed not from the Temple, but served God with fastings and prayers night and day. And she, coming in that instant, gave thanks likewise unto the Lord.

Explanatory Notes

[1] Passed. [2] The Law of Moses ordered all boy babies to be circumcised on the eighth day after birth; see Leviticus 12:1-3. [3] Meaning Savior. [4] Lasting forty days after a male child was born; see Leviticus 12:2-4. [5] Mo'-ses. [6] Je-ru'-sa-lem. [7] Commanded in Leviticus 12:8. [8] Consisting of a pair of turtle doves or two young pigeons; see Leviticus 12:6. [9] Sim'-e-on. [10] God-fearing. [11] The promised Savior. [12] Is'-ra-el. [13] Told. [14] Die happy. [15] Those not Jewish.

"Mine eyes have seen Thy salvation"

Bible Text

When the fullness of the time was come, God sent forth His Son, made of a woman, made under the Law. — *Galatians 4:4.*

Hymn

Come and worship, come and worship;
Worship Christ, the new-born King.

7. The Wise Men from the East

Now, when Jesus was born in Bethlehem,[1] behold, there came wise men[2] from the East[3] to Jerusalem,[4] saying, "Where is He that is born King of the Jews? For we have seen His star in the East and are come to worship Him."

When Herod,[5] the king, had heard these things, he was troubled[6] and all Jerusalem with him. And when he had gathered all the chief priests and scribes[7] of the people together, he demanded of them where Christ should be born. And they said unto him, "In Bethlehem of Judea; [8] for thus it is written by the Prophet, 'And thou, Bethlehem, in the land of Judah,[9] art not the least among the princes[10] of Judah; for out of thee shall come a Governor that shall rule My people Israel.' " [11]

Then Herod, when he had privily[12] called the Wise Men, inquired of them diligently what time the star appeared. And he sent them to Bethlehem and said, "Go and search diligently for the young Child; and when ye have found Him, bring me word again that I may come and worship Him also."

When they had heard the king, they departed; and, lo, the star which they saw in the East went before them till it came and stood over where the young Child was. When they saw the star, they rejoiced. And when they were come into the house, they saw the young Child with Mary, His mother, and fell down, and worshiped Him; and they presented unto Him gifts: gold, frankincense,[13] and myrrh.[14]

And being warned of God in a dream that they should not return to Herod, they departed into their country another way.

Explanatory Notes

[1] Beth'-le-hem. [2] Learned men, also called Magi. Thus Simeon's words that Jesus should be "a light to lighten the Gentiles" were already being fulfilled. [3] East of Palestine. [4] Je-ru'-sa-lem. [5] Her'-od. [6] Worried. [7] Those who copied the Scriptures. [8] Ju-de'-a. [9] Ju'-dah. [10] Chief cities. [11] Is'-ra-el. [12] Secretly. [13] Costly perfume; see Exodus 30: 34. [14] Gum from the sap of a tree; see Exodus 30: 23.

"They fell down and worshiped Him"

Bible Text

The Gentiles shall come to Thy light and kings to the brightness of Thy rising. — *Isaiah 60:3.*

Prayer

Lord God Holy Ghost, grant that many may accept Thy Word and come to faith in the Savior Jesus Christ. Amen.

8. The Flight to Egypt[1]

And when they[2] were departed, behold, the angel of the Lord appeareth to Joseph[3] in a dream, saying, "Arise and take the young Child and His mother and flee into Egypt, and be thou there until I bring thee word; for Herod will seek the young Child to destroy Him." [4]

When he arose, he took the young Child and His mother by night and departed into Egypt and was there until the death of Herod, that it might be fulfilled which was spoken of the Lord by the Prophet, saying, "Out of Egypt have I called My Son." [5]

Then Herod, when he saw that he was mocked[6] of the Wise Men, was exceeding wroth[7] and sent forth and slew[8] all the children that were in Bethlehem[9] and in all the coasts[10] thereof, from two years old and under, according to the time which he had diligently inquired of the Wise Men.

But when Herod was dead, behold, an angel of the Lord appeareth in a dream to Joseph in Egypt, saying, "Arise and take the young Child and His mother and go into the land of Israel; [11] for they are dead which sought the young Child's life."

And he arose and took the young Child and His mother and came into the land of Israel and dwelt[12] in a city called Nazareth[13] that it might be fulfilled which was spoken by the Prophets, "He shall be called a Nazarene."

Explanatory Notes

[1] E'-gypt. [2] The Wise Men. [3] Jo'-seph. . [4] Jesus had come into this sinful world to help and redeem all men; for all men are sinners. When He was born in Bethlehem, only few people came to greet and honor Him; and very soon some showed themselves as His bitter enemies and even wanted to kill Him. Herod was one of these. [5] See Hosea 11:1. [6] Fooled. [7] Very angry. [8] Killed. [9] Beth'-le-hem. [10] Region round about. [11] Is'-ra-el. [12] Lived. [13] Naz'-a-reth.

"And departed into Egypt"

Bible Text

I called My Son out of Egypt. — *Hosea 11:1.*

Prayer

Dear Savior, defend us and all who are in danger, and let not wicked people harm Thy children on earth. Amen.

9. The Twelve-Year-Old Jesus in the Temple[1]

Now, His parents went to Jerusalem[2] every year at the feast of the Passover.[3] And when He was twelve years old, they went up to Jerusalem after the custom of the feast. And when they had fulfilled the days,[4] as they returned, the Child Jesus tarried[5] behind in Jerusalem, and Joseph and His mother knew not of it. But they, supposing Him to have been in the company,[6] went a day's journey; and they sought Him among their kinsfolk[7] and acquaintance. And when they found Him not, they turned back again to Jerusalem, seeking Him.

And it came to pass that after three days they found Him in the Temple, sitting in the midst of the doctors,[8] both hearing them and asking them questions. And all that heard Him were astonished[9] at His understanding and answers. And when they saw Him, they were amazed.[10] And His mother said unto Him, "Son, why hast Thou thus dealt[11] with us? Behold, Thy father and I have sought Thee sorrowing."

And He said unto them, "How is it that ye sought Me? Wist[12] ye not that I must be about My Father's business?"

And they understood not the saying which He spake.

And He went down with them and came to Nazareth[13] and was subject[14] unto them; but His mother kept all these sayings in her heart.

And Jesus increased[15] in wisdom and stature[16] and in favor with[17] God and man.

Explanatory Notes

[1] Jesus grew to be a boy of school age in Nazareth. This is the only story in the Bible which tells us something about the Savior while He was a boy of that age. [2] Je-ru'-sa-lem. [3] One of the three great festivals of the Jews, also known as the Feast of Unleavened Bread. [4] When the seven days of the feast were over. [5] Stayed. [6] People who had traveled with them. [7] Relatives. [8] Learned men. [9] Greatly surprised. [10] Did not know what to think. [11] Treated us this way. [12] Knew. [13] Naz'-a-reth. [14] Obedient. [15] Grew. [16] Size and age. [17] Was well liked by.

"After three days they found Him in the Temple"

Bible Text

In Christ are hid all the treasures of wisdom and knowledge. — *Colossians 2:3.*

Prayer

Dear God, help us to love Thy Word as Jesus did, and help us likewise to be obedient to our parents. Amen.

10. The Preaching of John the Baptist

The word of God came unto John the Baptist[1] in the wilderness[2] of Judea.[3] And he came into all the country about Jordan,[4] preaching, "Repent ye,[5] for the kingdom of heaven is at hand." And John was clothed with camel's hair and a leathern girdle[6] about his loins;[7] and he did eat locusts[8] and wild honey. Then went out to him Jerusalem[9] and all Judea and all the region round about Jordan, and were baptized of him in Jordan, confessing their sins.

And the people mused[10] in their hearts of John whether he were the Christ or not; the Jews sent priests from Jerusalem to ask him, "Who art thou?" And he denied not but confessed, "I am not the Christ."

And they asked him, "Who then? Art thou Elias?" [11] And he saith, "I am not." "Art thou that Prophet?" And he answered, "No."

Then they said unto him, "Who art thou? What sayest thou of thyself?"

He said, "I am the voice of one crying in the wilderness, 'Make straight the way of the Lord,' as said the Prophet Esaias." [12]

And they asked him and said unto him, "Why baptizest thou, then, if thou be not Christ, nor Elias, neither that Prophet?"

John answered them, saying, "I indeed baptize you with water; but there standeth One among you whom ye know not. He it is who, coming after me, is mightier than I; whose shoes I am not worthy to stoop down and unloose. He shall baptize you with the Holy Ghost."

Explanatory Notes

[1] Jesus was about thirty years old and ready to make Himself known as the Savior. John the Baptist was Jesus' forerunner, who prepared His way. [2] The region along the Jordan and near the Dead Sea. [3] Ju-de′-a. [4] Jor′-dan. [5] Turn from your sins. [6] Belt. [7] Hips. [8] Grasshopperlike insects, which are eaten today in some regions. [9] Je-ru′-sa-lem. [10] Thought. [11] E-li′-as. [12] E-sa′-ias; Isaiah 40:3.

"Repent ye!"

Bible Text

The voice of him that crieth in the wilderness, "Prepare ye the way of the Lord." — *Isaiah 40:3*.

Prayer

Dear Lord Jesus Christ, give us faithful pastors, teachers, and missionaries who are filled with love for Thee, and use them to bring many to repentance and faith. Amen.

11. The Baptism of Jesus — The First Disciples [1]

Now, when all the people were baptized, then cometh Jesus from Galilee[2] to Jordan[3] unto John to be baptized of him. But John forbade[4] Him, saying, "I have need to be baptized of Thee, and comest Thou to me?" And Jesus, answering, said unto him, "Suffer[5] it to be so now; for thus it becometh Us[6] to fulfill all righteousness."[7] Then he suffered Him.

And Jesus, when He was baptized, went up straightway[8] out of the water and prayed; and, lo, the heavens were opened, and the Holy Ghost descended[9] like a dove upon Him; and a voice came from heaven, which said, "This is My beloved Son, in whom I am well pleased."

The next day after, John stood and two of his disciples; and looking upon Jesus as He walked, he saith, "Behold, the Lamb of God!" And the two disciples heard him speak, and they followed Jesus. One of the two was Andrew,[10] Simon Peter's brother. He first findeth his own brother Simon and saith unto him, "We have found the Messias."[11] And he brought him to Jesus. The day following, Jesus findeth Philip and saith unto him, "Follow Me." Philip findeth Nathanael[12] and saith unto him: "We have found Him of whom Moses in the Law and the Prophets did write, Jesus of Nazareth.[13] Come and see." Jesus saw Nathanael coming to Him and saith, "Behold an Israelite[14] indeed in whom is no guile."[15] Nathanael saith unto Him, "Whence knowest Thou me?" Jesus answered and said unto him, "Before that Philip called thee, when thou wast under the fig tree, I saw thee." Nathanael answered and saith unto Him, "Rabbi,[16] Thou art the Son of God; Thou art the King of Israel."

Explanatory Notes

[1] Pupils who believed in Jesus and followed Him. [2] Gal'-i-lee.
[3] Jor'-dan. [4] Refused. [5] Let. [6] It is our duty. [7] Do God's will. [8] At once. [9] Came down. [10] An'-drew. [11] The promised Savior. [12] Nathan'-a-el. [13] Naz'-a-reth. [14] Is'-ra-el-ite. [15] Who is true and honest. [16] Master.

"This is My beloved Son"

Bible Text

God hath made Him to be sin for us who knew no sin that we might be made the righteousness of God in Him. — *2 Corinthians 5:21.*

Prayer

Dear Jesus, grant that we may always be Thy disciples. Send Thy Holy Spirit into our hearts and keep us unto life eternal; for Thine own sake. Amen.

12. The Temptation of Jesus[1]

Then was Jesus led up of the Spirit into the wilderness to be tempted[2] of the devil. And when He had fasted[3] forty days and forty nights, He afterward hungered. And when the Tempter came to Him, he said, "If Thou be the Son of God, command that these stones be made bread."

But He answered and said, "It is written, 'Man shall not live by bread alone, but by every word that proceedeth[4] out of the mouth of God.' "

Then the devil taketh Him up into the Holy City[5] and setteth Him on a pinnacle[6] of the Temple and saith unto Him, "If Thou be the Son of God, cast Thyself down; for it is written, 'He shall give His angels charge concerning thee; and in their hands they shall bear thee up, lest at any time thou dash thy foot against a stone.' "

Jesus said unto Him, "It is written again, 'Thou shalt not tempt the Lord, thy God.' "

Again, the devil taketh Him up into an exceeding[7] high mountain and showeth Him all the kingdoms of the world and the glory of them; and saith unto Him, "All these things will I give Thee if Thou wilt fall down and worship[8] me."

Then saith Jesus unto him, "Get thee hence,[9] Satan! For it is written, 'Thou shalt worship the Lord, thy God, and Him only shalt thou serve.' "

Then the devil leaveth Him, and, behold, angels came and ministered[10] unto Him.

Explanatory Notes

[1] The devil knew that Jesus had come to redeem man from his power. When the Savior was about to begin this great work, Satan believed he might still spoil and hinder it. Therefore he tempted Jesus to sin, as he had tempted Adam and Eve and still tempts us. The temptation of Jesus followed His baptism and occurred before the choosing of His first five disciples. [2] Tried, tested. [3] Had not taken any food. [4] Goes. [5] Je-ru'-sa-lem. [6] The highest part of the roof. [7] Very. [8] Honor, pray to. [9] Away. [10] Served.

"Thou shalt worship the Lord, thy God"

Bible Text

He was in all points tempted like as we are, yet without sin. — *Hebrews 4:15.*

Hymn

The old evil Foe
Now means deadly woe;
Deep guile and great might
Are his dread arms in fight;
On earth is not his equal.

135

13. The Marriage in Cana[1]

And the third day there was a marriage in Cana of Galilee;[2] and the mother of Jesus was there; and both Jesus was called,[3] and His disciples, to the marriage.

When they wanted[4] wine, the mother of Jesus saith unto Him, "They have no wine."

Jesus saith unto her, "Woman, what have I to do with thee? Mine hour is not yet come."

His mother saith unto the servants, "Whatsoever He saith unto you, do it."

And there were set there six waterpots of stone, after the manner of the purifying[5] of the Jews, containing two or three firkins apiece.[6] Jesus saith unto them, "Fill the waterpots with water."

And they filled them up to the brim.

And He saith unto them, "Draw out now and bear it to the governor[7] of the feast."

And they bare it.

When the ruler of the feast had tasted the water that was made wine and knew not whence[8] it was (but the servants which drew the water knew), the governor of the feast called the bridegroom and saith unto him, "Every man at the beginning doth set forth good wine, and when men have well drunk, then that which is worse; but thou hast kept the good wine until now."

This beginning of miracles[9] did Jesus in Cana of Galilee and manifested[10] forth His glory; and His disciples believed[11] on Him.

Explanatory Notes

[1] Ca'-na. [2] Gal'-i-lee. [3] Invited. [4] Needed, lacked. [5] Washing or cleaning; see Numbers 31: 23-24. [6] Each pot held about 20 or 30 gallons. [7] Chief steward, who had charge of the feast. [8] From where. [9] Wonderful events produced by divine power. [10] Showed. [11] Their faith was strengthened, and they believed Jesus to be the Son of God.

"Fill the waterpots with water"

Bible Text

The Word was made flesh and dwelt among us; and we beheld
His glory, the glory as of the Only-begotten of the Father, full of
grace and truth. — *John 1:14.*

Prayer

Lord Jesus, we believe that Thou art the Son of God and the
Savior of the world. Keep us in this faith unto life everlasting. Amen.

14. Peter's Draught of Fishes

It came to pass that, as the people pressed[1] upon Him to hear the Word of God, He stood by the Lake of Gennesaret;[2] and He saw two ships standing by the lake, but the fishermen were gone out of them and were washing their nets. And He entered into one of the ships, which was Simon's,[3] and prayed him that he would thrust[4] out a little from the land. And He sat down and taught the people out of the ship.[5]

Now, when He had left speaking, He said unto Simon, "Launch[6] out into the deep[7] and let down your nets for a draught."[8]

And Simon, answering, said unto Him, "Master, we have toiled[9] all the night and have taken nothing; nevertheless, at Thy word I will let down the net." And when they had done this, they inclosed[10] a great multitude[11] of fishes; and their net brake. And they beckoned[12] unto their partners, which were in the other ship, that they should come and help them. And they came and filled both the ships, so that they began to sink.

When Simon Peter saw it, he fell down at Jesus' knees, saying, "Depart[13] from me; for I am a sinful man, O Lord." For he was astonished, and all that were with him, at the draught of the fishes which they had taken; and so was also James and John, which were partners with Simon.

Jesus said unto Simon, "Fear not; from henceforth[14] thou shalt catch men."

When they had brought their ships to land, they forsook[15] all and followed Him.

Explanatory Notes

[1] Crowded. [2] Gen-nes'-a-ret. [3] Si'-mon. [4] Push. [5] Wherever Jesus was seen, people gathered around Him in large numbers. He taught them, and more and more some became convinced that He was the promised Messiah. [6] Row. [7] Away from the shore, toward the middle of the lake. [8] A catch of fishes. [9] Worked hard. [10] Caught in the net. [11] Large number. [12] Waved with the hand. [13] Go away. [14] From now on. [15] Left.

"They inclosed a great multitude of fishes"

Bible Text

It is vain for you to rise up early, to sit up late, to eat the bread of sorrows; for so He giveth His beloved sleep. — *Psalm 127:2.*

Prayer

Dear Savior, help us more and more to love Thy Word and to hear and learn it gladly. Amen.

15. The Stilling of the Tempest[1]

The same day,[2] when the even was come, He saith unto them, "Let us pass over unto the other side of the lake."[3] And they launched forth.[4] But as they sailed, He fell asleep.

And, behold, there arose a great storm of wind, and the waves beat into the ship so that it was now full. And he was in the hinder[5] part of the ship, asleep on a pillow.

And His disciples came unto Him and awoke Him, saying, "Lord, save us, we perish!"[6]

And He saith unto them, "Why are ye so fearful? How is it that ye have no faith?" Then He arose and rebuked[7] the wind and the raging of the water and said unto the sea, "Peace, be still!" And the wind ceased,[8] and there was a great calm.[9]

But the men marveled,[10] saying one to another, "What manner of man is this that even the winds and the sea obey Him!"[11]

Explanatory Notes

[1] The quieting of the storm. [2] It had been a busy day for the Lord, a day of much teaching and preaching. His disciples had learned more about the kingdom of God, and a large crowd of people had again listened to His words of heavenly wisdom. Jesus was very tired from a hard day's work and longed for a rest, which shows that He was a true man. But at the same time He was the almighty God Himself, as the disciples were to see. [3] The Lake of Gennesaret, or the Sea of Galilee, where Peter had taken the great draught of fishes. [4] Set out. [5] Rear or back. [6] Die. [7] Commanded it to stop blowing and raging. [8] Stopped at once. [9] Instantly the sea was smooth. [10] Wondered. [11] The disciples could tell that Jesus was more than man, that He was God.

> Jesus, Lover of my soul,
>   Let me to Thy bosom fly
> While the nearer waters roll,
>   While the tempest still is high.
> Hide me, O my Savior, hide,
>   Till the storm of life is past;
> Safe into the haven guide,
>   Oh, receive my soul at last.

"Peace, be still!"

Bible Text

All power is given unto Me in heaven and in earth. — *Matthew 28:18.*

Prayer

Lord Jesus, we believe that Thou art the almighty Son of God. Grant that we may ever trust in Thee. Amen.

16. The Man Sick of the Palsy

And He entered into a ship and passed over and came into His own city.[1] And, behold, they brought to Him a man sick of the palsy,[2] lying upon a bed, which was borne[3] by four. And when they could not come nigh[4] unto Him for the press,[5] they uncovered the roof where He was and let down the bed wherein the sick of the palsy lay. And Jesus, seeing their faith, said unto the sick of the palsy, "Son, be of good cheer; thy sins be forgiven thee."

And, behold, certain of the scribes[6] said within themselves, "This man blasphemeth.[7] Who can forgive sins but God only?"

Jesus, knowing their thoughts, said, "Wherefore think ye evil in your hearts? For whether[8] is easier, to say, 'Thy sins be forgiven thee,' or to say, 'Arise and walk'? But that ye may know that the Son of Man hath power on earth to forgive sins," then saith He to the man sick of the palsy, "Arise, take up thy bed, and go unto thine house."

And he arose and departed to his house.

But when the multitude[9] saw it, they marveled,[10] and glorified[11] God, which had given such power unto men.

Explanatory Notes

[1] "His own city" was Capernaum, where Jesus had made His home. He had been on the other side of the Sea of Galilee, in the land of the Gadarenes and Gergesenes. But the people there did not welcome Him, for, after He had driven devils out of two men, they asked Jesus to leave their country. So the Lord and His disciples returned to Capernaum. This story shows us how differently the people there acted, and how He proved to them still more that He was the Son of God. [2] A painful paralysis, in which the patient cannot move the limbs. [3] Carried. [4] Near. [5] Mass of people crowding around Jesus. [6] Learned teachers who copied the Law. [7] Mocks God. [8] Which of the two. [9] All the people. [10] Wondered at Jesus' great power. [11] Praised.

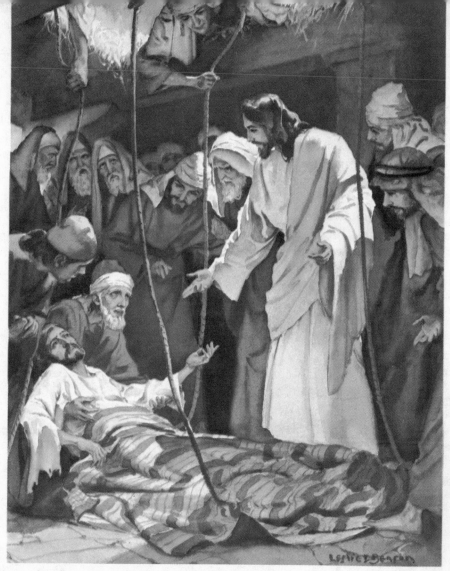

"Be of good cheer; thy sins be forgiven thee"

Bible Text

This is the true God and eternal life. — *1 John 5:20.*

Hymn

Forget not Him whose meekness
    Still bears with all Thy sin,
Who healeth all thy weakness,
    Renews thy life within.

17. The Daughter of Jairus[1]

And, behold, there came a man named Jairus, a ruler of the synagog;[2] and he fell down at Jesus' feet and besought[3] Him that He would come into his house; for he had one only daughter, about twelve years of age, and she lay a-dying. But as He went, there cometh one from the ruler of the synagog's house, saying to him, "Thy daughter is dead; trouble not the Master." But when Jesus heard it, He answered him, saying, "Fear not, only believe, and she shall be made whole." [4]

And when Jesus came into the ruler's house and saw the minstrels[5] and the people making a noise,[6] He said unto them, "Give place;[7] for the maid is not dead, but sleepeth." And they laughed Him to scorn.

But when the people were put forth, He went in and took her by the hand and said unto her, "Damsel, I say unto thee, Arise." And straightway the damsel arose and walked; and He commanded to give her meat.[8] And the fame hereof[9] went abroad into all that land.

The Young Man of Nain[10]

And He went into a city called Nain; and many of His disciples went with Him, and much people. When He came nigh unto the gate of the city, behold, there was a dead man carried out, the only son of his mother, and she was a widow.

The Lord had compassion[11] on her and said unto her, "Weep not." And He came and touched the bier;[12] and they that bare[13] him stood still. And He said, "Young man, I say unto thee, Arise." And he that was dead sat up and began to speak. And He delivered him to his mother.

And they glorified God, saying, "A great prophet is risen up among us; God hath visited His people."

Explanatory Notes

[1] Ja-i′-rus. [2] Officer in a Jewish church. [3] Begged. [4] Alive and healthy. [5] Players of sad music. [6] Wailing and weeping. [7] Make room. [8] Food. [9] The story. [10] Na′-in. [11] Pity. [12] Coffin. [13] Carried.

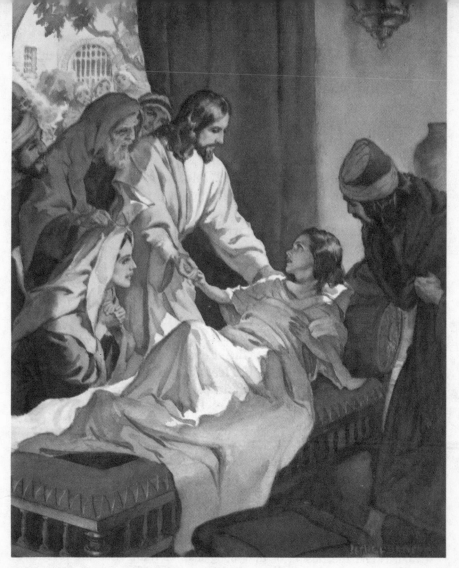

"I say unto thee, Arise"

Bible Text

I am the Resurrection and the Life. — *John 11:25.*

Hymn

Jesus, my Redeemer, lives;
I too unto life shall waken.

18. The Centurion of Capernaum[1]

And when Jesus was entered into Capernaum,[2] there came unto Him a centurion,[3] beseeching[4] Him and saying, "Lord, my servant lieth at home sick of the palsy,[5] grievously tormented."[6]

And Jesus saith unto him, "I will come and heal him."

The centurion answered and said, "Lord, I am not worthy that Thou shouldest come under my roof; but speak the word only, and my servant shall be healed. For I am a man under authority[7] having soldiers under me; and I say unto this man, 'Go,' and he goeth; and to another, 'Come,' and he cometh; and to my servant, 'Do this,' and he doeth it."

When Jesus heard it, He marveled and said to them that followed, "Verily,[8] I say unto you, I have not found so great faith, no, not in Israel.[9] And I say unto you, That many shall come from the East and West and shall sit down with Abraham[10] and Isaac[11] and Jacob[12] in the kingdom of heaven. But the children of the Kingdom shall be cast out into outer darkness; there shall be weeping and gnashing of teeth."

And Jesus said unto the centurion, "Go thy way; and as thou hast believed, so be it done unto thee."

And his servant was healed in the selfsame hour.

Explanatory Notes

[1] This story occurred between the raising of the daughter of Jairus and the raising of the young man of Nain. See the preceding story, No. 17. Jesus had preached His powerful Sermon on the Mount to a large number of people (Matthew 5-7) and was now returning to Capernaum. [2] Ca-per'-na-um. [3] Captain of one hundred men in the Roman army. [4] Pleading with Him. [5] A very painful paralysis in which the sufferer cannot move his limbs. [6] Suffering very great pain. [7] I must obey orders of those above me. [8] Surely, or truly. [9] Is'-ra-el. [10] A'-bra-ham. [11] I'-saac. [12] Ja'-cob.

Jesus, Thou art all compassion,
Pure, unbounded love Thou art;
Visit us with Thy salvation,
Enter every trembling heart.

"There came a centurion, beseeching Him"

Bible Text

God is no respecter of persons; but in every nation he that feareth Him and worketh righteousness is accepted with Him. — *Acts 10:34-35.*

Hymn

Have we trials and temptations?
Is there trouble anywhere?
We should never be discouraged —
Take it to the Lord in prayer.

19. Death of John the Baptist

Herod[1] had sent forth and laid hold upon John; and he bound him and put him in prison for Herodias'[2] sake, his brother Philip's wife; for he had married her. For John said unto him, "It is not lawful for thee to have her."[3] When he would have put him to death, he feared the multitude, because they counted[4] him as a prophet.

But when Herod's birthday was kept,[5] the daughter of Herodias came in and danced and pleased Herod and them that sat with him. And the king said unto the damsel,[6] "Ask of me whatsoever thou wilt, and I will give it thee." And he sware[7] unto her, "Whatsoever thou shalt ask of me, I will give it thee, unto the half of my kingdom."

And she went forth and said unto her mother, "What shall I ask?"

She said, "The head of John the Baptist."

And she came in straightway with haste[8] unto the king and asked, saying, "I will that thou give me in a charger[9] the head of John the Baptist."

And the king was exceeding sorry; yet for his oath's[10] sake and them which sat with him, he would not reject[11] her. And immediately the king sent an executioner;[12] and he beheaded him in the prison and brought his head in a charger and gave it to the damsel, and the damsel gave it to her mother.

And his disciples came and took up the body and buried it, and went and told Jesus.

Explanatory Notes

[1] Her'-od. [2] He-ro'-di-as. [3] John the Baptist was a fearless preacher. When King Herod sent away his own wife and married the wife of his brother, John bravely told the king that he had committed a great sin. It made no difference to John whether the king liked this or not. He preached the truth no matter what would happen to him. [4] Looked upon. [5] Celebrated. [6] Young woman. [7] Promised by swearing an oath. [8] In a hurry, before Herod would change his mind. [9] Large dish. [10] What he had sworn. [11] Refuse. [12] Officer who puts criminals to death.

"And immediately the king sent an executioner"

Bible Text

Be thou faithful unto death, and I will give thee a crown of life. — *Revelation 2:10.*

Prayer

Lord God, Holy Ghost, strengthen our faith and keep us faithful unto death; for Jesus' sake. Amen

20. Feeding of the Five Thousand

Jesus went over the Sea of Galilee.[1] A great multitude[2] followed Him because they saw His miracles which He did on them that were diseased.[3] And Jesus went up into a mountain, and there He sat with His disciples.

When Jesus then lifted up His eyes and saw a great company come unto Him, He saith unto Philip, "Whence[4] shall we buy bread that these may eat?" This He said to prove[5] him; for He Himself knew what He would do.

Philip answered Him, "Two hundred pennyworth[6] of bread is not sufficient[7] for them that every one of them may take a little."

Andrew[8] saith unto Him, "There is a lad here which hath five barley loaves and two small fishes; but what are they among so many?"

And Jesus said, "Make the men sit down." Now, there was much grass in that place. So the men sat down, in number about five thousand.[9] And Jesus took the loaves; and when He had given thanks, He distributed[10] to the disciples and the disciples to them that were set down; and likewise of the fishes, as much as they would.[11]

When they were filled,[12] He said unto His disciples, "Gather up the fragments that remain[13] that nothing be lost."

Therefore they gathered them together and filled twelve baskets with the fragments of the five barley loaves which remained over and above unto them that had eaten.

Then those men, when they had seen the miracle that Jesus did, said, "This is of a truth that Prophet that should come into the world." [14]

Explanatory Notes

[1] Gal'-i-lee. [2] Large numbers of people. [3] Sick. [4] Wherefrom. [5] Try, or test. [6] About $40.00. [7] Enough. [8] An'-drew. [9] At another time Jesus fed four thousand. See Matthew 15:32-39 and Mark 8:1-9. [10] Handed out. [11] As much as everybody wanted. [12] Had satisfied their hunger. [13] Pieces left over. [14] The promised Savior and Messiah.

"He distributed to the disciples"

Bible Text

Seek ye first the kingdom of God and His righteousness, and all these things shall be added unto you. — *Matthew 6:33.*

Prayer

Lord God, heavenly Father, bless us and these Thy gifts which we receive from Thy bountiful goodness, through Jesus Christ, our Lord. Amen.

21. Jesus Walks on the Sea

When Jesus, therefore, perceived[1] that they would come and take Him by force to make Him a king,[2] He constrained[3] His disciples to get into a ship and to go before Him unto the other side. And when He had sent the multitudes away, He went up into a mountain apart to pray. And His disciples went down unto the sea and entered into a ship. And it was now dark, and Jesus was not come to them. And the sea arose by reason of a great wind that blew. But the ship was now in the midst of the sea, tossed[4] with waves.

And in the fourth watch[5] of the night Jesus went unto them, walking on the sea. And He would have passed by them. And when they saw Him walking on the sea, they were troubled, saying, "It is a spirit"; and they cried out for fear. But straightway Jesus spake unto them, saying, "Be of good cheer; it is I; be not afraid."

And Peter answered Him and said, "Lord, if it be Thou, bid me come unto Thee on the water." And He said, "Come." And when Peter was come down out of the ship, he walked on the water to go to Jesus. But when he saw the wind boisterous,[6] he was afraid; and beginning to sink, he cried, "Lord, save me!" And immediately Jesus stretched forth His hand and caught him and said unto him, "O thou of little faith, wherefore didst thou doubt?"

And when they were come into the ship, the wind ceased.[7] And immediately the ship was at the land whither[8] they went. Then they that were in the ship came and worshiped Him, saying, "Of a truth Thou art the Son of God."

Explanatory Notes

[1] Saw. [2] After Jesus had fed the five thousand, some of them wanted to make Him their earthly king. Jesus wanted the people to accept Him as their heavenly King, the Savior from sin. [3] Urged. [4] Thrown about. [5] Between three and six o'clock in the morning. [6] A large roaring wave came toward him. [7] Stopped. [8] To which.

"Jesus stretched forth His hand and caught him"

Bible Text

Be not afraid, only believe. — *Mark 5:36.*

Hymn

Lord Jesus, who dost love me,
Oh, spread Thy wings above me
And shield me from alarm!

22. The Woman of Canaan[1]

Then Jesus departed into the coasts[2] of Tyre and Sidon.[3] And behold, a woman of Canaan,[4] a Greek, came out of the same coasts and cried unto Him, saying, "Have mercy on me, O Lord, Thou Son of David![5] My daughter is grievously vexed[6] with a devil."

But He answered her not a word.

And His disciples came and besought[7] Him, saying, "Send her away; for she crieth after us."

But He answered and said, "I am not sent but unto the lost sheep of the house of Israel."[8]

Then came she and worshiped Him, saying, "Lord, help me!"

But He answered and said, "It is not meet[9] to take the children's bread and to cast[10] it to the dogs."

And she said, "Truth,[11] Lord; yet the dogs eat of the crumbs which fall from their masters' table."

Then Jesus answered and said unto her, "O woman, great is thy faith; be it unto thee even as thou wilt."

And her daughter was made whole[12] from that very hour.

Explanatory Notes

[1] While the Lord Jesus lived on earth among the people, He was greatly surprised only a few times. once because of men's unbelief (Mark 6:6) and twice at the remarkable faith which certain persons showed. The first of these was the centurion of Capernaum (No. 18), the second the woman of Canaan. [2] Region. [3] Si'-don. [4] Ca'-naan. [5] Da'-vid. [6] Greatly troubled and made to suffer severely. [7] Begged. [8] Is'-ra-el. [9] Proper. [10] Throw. [11] That is true. [12] Healthy and strong.

> Approach, my soul, the mercy seat
> Where Jesus answers prayer;
> There humbly fall before His feet,
> For none can perish there.

"Lord, help me!"

Bible Text

What things soever ye desire, when ye pray, believe that ye receive them, and ye shall have them. — *Mark 11:24.*

Hymn

What a Friend we have in Jesus,
　All our sins and griefs to bear!
What a privilege to carry
　Everything to God in prayer!

23. Mary and Martha[1]

Now, it came to pass, as they went, that He entered into a certain village;[2] and a certain woman, named Martha, received Him into her house.

And she had a sister, called Mary, which also sat at Jesus' feet and heard His Word.

But Martha was cumbered[3] about much serving[4] and came to Him and said, "Lord, dost Thou not care that my sister hath left me to serve alone? Bid her therefore that she help me."

And Jesus answered and said unto her, "Martha, Martha, thou art careful[5] and troubled about many things; but one thing is needful.[6] And Mary hath chosen that good part,[7] which shall not be taken away from her."

Explanatory Notes

[1] Among the very close friends of Jesus were the two sisters Martha and Mary and their brother Lazarus. They lived in the little village of Bethany, not far from Jerusalem. In the house of these people Jesus was an ever welcome guest. Now Jesus again stops at the home of these friends. We see how happy they are to have the Lord in their house and how each of them is trying to serve Him in her own way. We see also how Jesus teaches the two sisters a most important lesson during His visit. [2] The village of Bethany. [3] Worried and troubled. [4] She thought she could serve Jesus best by making a meal for Him and by otherwise making His stay as comfortable as possible. [5] Anxious or worried. [6] Necessary above everything else. [7] Here Jesus indicates that hearing the Word of God is the most important thing of all.

How were Mary's thoughts devoted
    Her eternal joy to find
As intent each word she noted,
    At her Savior's feet reclined! —
For Jesus all earthly concerns she forgot,
And all was repaid in that one happy lot.

"Mary hath chosen that good part"

Bible Text

Blessed are they that hear the Word of God and keep it. — *Luke 11:28.*

Prayer

Dear Savior, grant that we may hold Thy Word sacred and that we may gladly hear and learn it. Amen.

24. Jesus Blessing Little Children[1]

The disciples came unto Jesus, saying, "Who is the greatest in the kingdom of heaven?" [2]

And Jesus called a little child unto Him and set him in the midst of them and said, "Verily I say unto you, Except ye be converted[3] and become as little children, ye shall not enter into the kingdom of heaven. Whosoever, therefore, shall humble[4] himself as this little child, the same is greatest in the kingdom of heaven. And whoso shall receive one such little child in My name receiveth Me: But whoso shall offend[5] one of these little ones which believe in Me, it were better for him that a millstone were hanged about his neck and that he were drowned in the depth of the sea. Take heed[6] that ye despise[7] not one of these little ones; for I say unto you that in heaven their angels do always behold the face of My Father which is in heaven."

And they brought young children to Him that He should touch them; [8] and His disciples rebuked[9] those that brought them. But when Jesus saw it, He was much displeased and said unto them, "Suffer[10] the little children to come unto Me and forbid them not; for of such is the kingdom of God. Verily I say unto you, Whosoever shall not receive the kingdom of God as a little child, he shall not enter therein." And He took them up in His arms, put His hands upon them, and blessed them.

Explanatory Notes

[1] Jesus, the Savior, is the Friend in particular of little children. How highly He thinks of them, and how dearly He loves them, is shown here. [2] Before this, the disciples had quarreled among themselves which of them would be given the highest place in heaven. [3] Unless you are changed into believers. [4] Lower. [5] Do anything to cause a child to sin. [6] Take care. [7] Look down on, or think little of. [8] Lay His hands upon them and bless them. [9] Scolded. [10] Permit.

"He took them up in His arms"

Bible Text

Out of the mouth of babes and sucklings hast Thou ordained strength. — *Psalm 8:2.*

Hymn

Gracious Savior, gentle Shepherd. Children all are dear to Thee;
Gathered with Thine arms and carried In Thy bosom may they be;
Sweetly, fondly, safely tended, From all harm and danger free.

25. The Raising of Lazarus[1]

Now, a certain man was sick, named Lazarus, of Bethany. Therefore his sisters, Mary and Martha, sent unto Jesus, saying, "Lord, behold, he whom Thou lovest is sick." And He abode[2] two days still in the same place where He was. After that He saith unto His disciples "Lazarus is dead; nevertheless let us go unto him."

When Jesus came, He found that he had lain in the grave four days already. Martha, as soon as she heard that Jesus was coming, went and met Him. Then said Martha unto Jesus, "Lord, if Thou hadst been here, my brother had not died." Jesus saith unto her, "Thy brother shall rise again." Martha saith unto Him, "I know that he shall rise again in the resurrection at the Last Day." Jesus said unto her, "I am the Resurrection and the Life; he that believeth in Me, though he were dead, yet shall he live; and whosoever liveth and believeth in Me shall never die. Believest thou this?" She said unto Him, "Yea, Lord; I believe that Thou art the Christ, the Son of God." Then, when Mary was come where Jesus was and saw Him, she fell down at His feet, saying unto Him, "Lord, if Thou hadst been here, my brother had not died."

Jesus cometh to the grave. It was a cave, and a stone lay upon it. Jesus said, "Take ye away the stone." Martha said unto Him, "Lord, by this time he stinketh; for he hath been dead four days." Jesus saith unto her, "Said I not unto thee that if thou wouldest believe, thou shouldest see the glory of God." Then they took away the stone. And Jesus lifted up His eyes and said, "Father, I thank Thee that Thou hast heard Me " And He cried with a loud voice, "Lazarus, come forth!" And he came forth, bound with graveclothes. Jesus saith, "Loose him and let him go."

Many of the Jews believed on Him. But the chief priests and the Pharisees took counsel[3] to put Him to death.

Explanatory Notes
[1] Laz'-a-rus. [2] Stayed. [3] Made plans.

"Loose him and let him go"

Bible Text

The hour is coming in the which all that are in the graves shall hear His voice and shall come forth. — *John 5:28-29.*

Prayer

Lord Jesus, we believe that Thou art the Son of God and the Savior of the world. Keep us in that faith unto death, and on the Last Day raise us unto life eternal. Amen.

161

26. Zacchaeus

Jesus entered and passed through Jericho.[2] And, behold, there was a man named Zacchaeus, which was the chief among the publicans,[3] and he was rich. And he sought to see Jesus who He was, and could not for the press,[4] because he was little of stature.[5] And he ran before[6] and climbed up into a sycamore tree to see Him; for He was to pass that way.

And when Jesus came to the place, He looked up and saw him and said unto him, "Zacchaeus, make haste and come down, for today I must abide[7] at thy house."

And he made haste and came down and received Him joyfully.

And when they[8] saw it, they all murmured,[9] saying that He was gone to be guest with a man that is a sinner.[10]

And Zacchaeus stood and said unto the Lord, "Behold, Lord, the half of my goods I give to the poor, and if I have taken anything from any man by false accusation,[11] I restore him fourfold." [12]

And Jesus said unto him, "This day is salvation[13] come to this house, forsomuch as he also is a son of Abraham.[14] For the Son of Man is come to seek and to save that which was lost."

Explanatory Notes

[1] Zac-chae'-us. [2] Jer'-i-cho. [3] Tax collectors, who were despised by most people because many of them were dishonest. [4] Crowd of people. [5] Size. [6] Ahead. [7] Stay for a while. [8] The self-righteous people, especially the scribes and Pharisees. [9] Grumbled. [10] Jesus very often showed Himself as the Friend of sinners. No matter how great a sinner a person had been, if he was truly sorry for what he had done and came to Jesus, He joyfully accepted him as one who had returned to his God, as a lost sheep which had been found again. The scribes and Pharisees objected to this mercy of Jesus. [11] In a dishonest way. [12] Return four times as much as I have taken. [13] Great blessing, forgiveness of sins. [14] A'-bra-ham.

"Zacchaeus, make haste and come down"

Bible Text

Christ Jesus came into the world to save sinners. — *1 Timothy 1:15.*

Prayer

Lord Jesus, I thank Thee that Thou hast redeemed me and made me Thine own; help me now to live for Thee and to serve Thee in thankfulness. Amen.

27. The Lost Sheep[1]

Then drew near unto Him all the publicans and sinners for to hear Him. And the Pharisees and scribes murmured, saying, "This man receiveth sinners and eateth[2] with them."

And He spake this parable unto them, saying:

"What man of you, having an hundred sheep, if he lose one of them, doth not leave the ninety and nine in the wilderness and go after that which is lost until he find it? And when he hath found it, he layeth it on his shoulders, rejoicing. And when he cometh home, he calleth together his friends and neighbors, saying unto them, 'Rejoice with me; for I have found my sheep which was lost.' I say unto you that likewise joy shall be in heaven over one sinner that repenteth, more than over ninety and nine just persons which need no repentance." [3]

Explanatory Notes

[1] This and the following four stories are so-called parables of our Lord. They are stories about things and happenings in this world which the people well understood. Jesus used these stories in teaching the people what He wanted them to learn about heaven and the kingdom of God. We might call parables earthly stories with heavenly meanings. [2] Jesus had accepted invitations to their houses and eaten meals there. [3] God wants all men to be saved. His wonderful love and mercy is beyond our understanding. He does not want a single person to be lost, no matter how great a sinner he may be or how far he may have strayed away from God.

The Lord's my Shepherd; I'll not want.
 He makes me down to lie
In pastures green; He leadeth me
 The quiet waters by.

My soul He doth restore again
 And me to walk doth make
Within the paths of righteousness
 E'en for His own name's sake.

"I have found my sheep"

Bible Text

The Son of Man is come to save that which was lost. — *Matthew 18:11.*

Hymn

Perverse and foolish, oft I strayed,
But yet in love He sought me
And on His shoulder gently laid
And home, rejoicing, brought me.

28. The Prodigal[1] Son

Jesus said:

A certain man had two sons. And the younger of them said to his father, "Father, give me the portion of goods that falleth[2] to me." And he divided unto them his living.[3] And not many days after, the younger son gathered all together and took his journey into a far country and there wasted his substance[4] with riotous living.[5]

And when he had spent all, there arose a mighty famine[6] in that land, and he began to be in want.[7] And he went and joined himself to a citizen of that country; and he sent him into his fields to feed swine. And he would fain[8] have filled his belly with husks[9] that the swine did eat, and no man gave unto him.

And when he came to himself,[10] he said, "How many hired servants of my father's have bread enough and to spare, and I perish with hunger! I will arise and go to my father and will say unto him, 'Father, I have sinned against Heaven and before thee and am no more worthy to be called thy son; make me as one of thy hired servants.' "

And he arose and came to his father. But when he was yet a great way off, his father saw him and had compassion[11] and ran and fell on his neck and kissed him. And the son said unto him, "Father, I have sinned against Heaven and in thy sight and am no more worthy to be called thy son." But the father said to his servants, "Bring forth the best robe[12] and put it on him, and put a ring on his hand and shoes on his feet, and bring hither the fatted calf and kill it, and let us eat and be merry; for this my son was dead and is alive again; he was lost and is found." And they began to be merry.

Explanatory Notes

[1] A prodigal is a wasteful person. [2] Will be mine some day. [3] All that he had. [4] Spent foolishly all that he had. [5] Sinful life. [6] Shortage of food. [7] Great need. [8] Gladly. [9] The pods of the carob tree. [10] Realizing what he had done. [11] Pity. [12] A white embroidered garment, worn on special occasions.

"His father had compassion"

Bible Text

Likewise, I say unto you, there is joy in the presence of the angels of God over one sinner that repenteth. — *Luke 15:10.*

Hymn

Assist my soul, too apt to stray,
A stricter watch to keep;
And should I e'er forget Thy way,
Restore Thy wandering sheep.

29. The Rich Man and Poor Lazarus[1]

There was a certain rich man, which was clothed in purple and fine linen and fared sumptuously[2] every day. And there was a certain beggar, named Lazarus, which was laid at his gate, full of sores and desiring to be fed with the crumbs which fell from the rich man's table; moreover, the dogs came and licked his sores.

And it came to pass that the beggar died and was carried by the angels into Abraham's[3] bosom.[4]

The rich man also died and was buried. And in hell he lifted up his eyes, being in torments,[5] and seeth Abraham afar off and Lazarus in his bosom. And he cried and said, "Father Abraham, have mercy on me and send Lazarus that he may dip the tip of his finger in water and cool my tongue; for I am tormented in this flame."

But Abraham said, "Son, remember that thou in thy lifetime receivedst thy good things and likewise Lazarus evil things; but now he is comforted,[6] and thou art tormented. And beside all this, between us and you there is a great gulf[7] fixed, so that they which would pass from hence to you cannot, neither can they pass to us that would come from thence."

Then he said, "I pray thee therefore, Father, that thou wouldest send him to my father's house, for I have five brethren, that he may testify[8] unto them lest they also come into this place of torment."

Abraham saith unto him, "They have Moses and the Prophets: let them hear them."

And he said, "Nay, Father Abraham; but if one went unto them from the dead, they will repent."

And he said unto him, "If they hear not Moses and the Prophets, neither will they be persuaded[9] though one rose from the dead."

Explanatory Notes

[1] Laz'-a-rus. [2] Ate and drank only the best to be had. [3] A'-bra-ham. [4] Glorious heaven. [5] Great pain. [6] Made happy. [7] A deep opening, or gap. [8] Tell and prove. [9] Made to believe.

"The dogs came and licked his sores"

Bible Text

Enter ye in at the strait gate; for wide is the gate, and broad is the way, that leadeth to destruction; and many there be which go in thereat. — *Matthew 7:13.*

Prayer

Lord Jesus, dear Savior, keep us unto life everlasting; for Thy mercy's sake. Amen.

30. The Pharisee and the Publican[1]

He spake this parable unto certain which trusted in themselves that they were righteous[2] and despised[3] others:

Two men went up into the Temple to pray, the one a Pharisee[4] and the other a publican.[5]

The Pharisee stood and prayed thus with himself: "God, I thank Thee that I am not as other men are: extortioners,[6] unjust, adulterers,[7] or even as this publican. I fast[8] twice in the week, I give tithes[9] of all that I possess."

And the publican, standing afar off, would not lift up so much as his eyes to heaven, but smote[10] upon his breast, saying, "God be merciful to me, a sinner."

I tell you, this man went down to his house justified[11] rather than the other; for every one that exalteth himself[12] shall be abased,[13] and he that humbleth himself[14] shall be exalted.

Explanatory Notes

[1] There is only one way to heaven, and that is by faith in Jesus, the Savior. However, many people wish to enter heaven in their own way. They believe that by their own good deeds they can please God so that He will accept them. These people are to be pitied, for they are blind and deceive themselves. Many of them will remain so and not notice their mistake until it is too late. There were such men also at the time of Jesus, and to these He told the parable of the Pharisee and the Publican. [2] Just and holy before God. [3] Looked down upon, disliked, and hated them. [4] One of the Jewish leaders, who considered themselves very righteous. [5] Tax collector, considered by most people as being very low and dishonest. [6] People v ho force money from others. [7] People who sin against the Sixth Commandment and break marriage. [8] Do not eat anything. [9] The tenth part. [10] Struck with his hand. [11] With his sins forgiven. [12] Thinks himself more than others. [13] Put to shame. [14] Considers himself low.

"Two men went up into the Temple to pray"

Bible Text

Therefore we conclude that a man is justified by faith, without the deeds of the Law. — *Romans 3:28.*

Hymn

Rock of Ages, cleft for me,
Let me hide myself in Thee!

31. The Good Samaritan[1]

And, behold, a certain lawyer stood up and tempted Him, saying, "Master, what shall I do to inherit eternal life?"

He said unto him, "What is written in the Law? How readest thou?"

And he, answering, said, "Thou shalt love the Lord, thy God, with all thy heart and with all thy soul and with all thy strength and with all thy mind, and thy neighbor as thyself."

And He said unto him, "Thou hast answered right. This do, and thou shalt live."

But he, willing to justify himself, said unto Jesus, "And who is my neighbor?"

And Jesus, answering, said, "A certain man went down from Jerusalem[2] to Jericho[3] and fell among thieves, which stripped him of his raiment[4] and wounded him and departed, leaving him half dead. And by chance there came down a certain priest that way; and when he saw him, he passed by on the other side. And likewise a Levite[5] came and looked on him and passed by on the other side.

"But a certain Samaritan,[6] as he journeyed,[7] came where he was; and he had compassion[8] on him and went to him and bound up his wounds, pouring in oil and wine, and set him on his own beast[9] and brought him to an inn[10] and took care of him. And on the morrow,[11] when he departed, he took out two pence[12] and gave them to the host[13] and said unto him, 'Take care of him, and whatsoever thou spendest more, when I come again, I will repay thee.'

"Which now of these three thinkest thou was neighbor unto him that fell among the thieves?"

And the lawyer said, "He that showed mercy unto him."

Then said Jesus unto him, "Go and do thou likewise."

Explanatory Notes

[1] Sa-mar'-i-tan. [2] Je-ru'-sa-lem. [3] Jer'-i-cho. [4] Clothes. [5] Le'-vite, an assistant priest. [6] Man from Samaria, who was despised by the Jews. [7] Traveled. [8] Pity. [9] Mule or horse. [10] Hotel. [11] Next day. [12] About 40 cents; a pence was a day's wages. [13] The hotel manager.

"He had compassion on him"

Bible Text

All things whatsoever ye would that men should do to you, do ye even so to them. — *Matthew 7:12.*

Prayer

Dear Father in heaven, fill us with love and pity for those who are in trouble and make us willing to help them; for Jesus' sake. Amen.

32. The Entry of Jesus into Jerusalem[1]

And when they drew nigh[2] unto Jerusalem[3] and were come to Bethphage,[4] unto the Mount of Olives, then sent Jesus two disciples, saying unto them, "Go into the village over against you, and straightway[5] ye shall find an ass[6] tied and a colt with her; loose them and bring them unto Me. And if any man say aught[7] unto you, ye shall say, 'The Lord hath need of them,' and straightway he will send them."

All this was done that it might be fulfilled which was spoken by the Prophet,[8] saying, "Tell ye the daughter of Zion,[9] 'Behold thy King cometh unto thee, meek[10] and sitting upon an ass, and a colt, the foal[11] of an ass.' "

And the disciples went and did as Jesus commanded them and brought the ass and the colt and put on them their clothes; and they set Him thereon.

And a very great multitude spread their garments in the way; others cut down branches from the trees and strewed[12] them in the way. And the multitude that went before and that followed, cried, saying, "Hosanna[13] to the Son of David! Blessed is He that cometh in the name of the Lord! Hosanna in the highest!"

Explanatory Notes

[1] Jesus and His disciples were now on the way to Jerusalem, where He was about to begin His great suffering, which ended in His death on the cross. [2] Came near. [3] Je-ru'-sa-lem. [4] Beth'-pha-ge. [5] Immediately. [6] Donkey. [7] Anything to stop you from taking the ass. [8] See Zechariah 9:9. [9] Zi'-on, the city of Jerusalem, which stands for the Christian Church. [10] Gentle, not proud. [11] The young. [12] Scattered. [13] The meaning of the word "hosanna" is, "Save, we beseech Thee." On this occasion it was also an exclamation of joy and praise.

"Hosanna in the highest!"
That ancient song we sing,
For Christ is our Redeemer,
The Lord of heaven our King.

"Thy King cometh unto thee"

Bible Text

Lift up your heads, O ye gates; and be ye lifted up, ye everlasting doors; and the King of Glory shall come in. — *Psalm 24:7.*

Prayer

Lord Jesus Christ, we believe that Thou art our God and Savior. Make our praises sincere and true, and keep us ever in Thy grace. Amen.

33. The Widow's Mites[1]

And Jesus sat over against the treasury[2] and beheld[3] how the people cast money into the treasury; and many that were rich cast in much. And there came a certain poor widow, and she threw in two mites, which make a farthing.[4]

And He called unto Him His disciples and saith unto them, "Verily I say unto you, That this poor widow hath cast more in than all they which have cast into the treasury; for they did all cast in of their abundance; [5] but she of her want[6] did cast in all that she had, even all her living." [7]

Explanatory Notes

[1] This story shows what the Lord thinks of our gifts, of the money which we bring for the poor, for missions, or for the purpose of keeping our church and school buildings in good condition. It shows that God does not only see how much we bring to Him, but that above all He looks into our hearts and notes with what kind of feeling we bring our gifts. [2] Jesus sat across from the treasury, where He could see how the people contributed for the kingdom of God. The treasury was a collection box in the Temple, into which people placed their gifts. [3] Saw. [4] A mite was the smallest copper coin used, worth about one eighth of a cent in American money. A farthing amounted to about one fourth of a cent. [5] They had money to spare, and their gifts were no sacrifice. [6] The poor widow had nothing except the two mites which she contributed. [7] All that she had, the money that she really needed to live on.

Grant us hearts, dear Lord, to yield Thee
   Gladly, freely, of Thine own;
With the sunshine of Thy goodness
   Melt our thankless hearts of stone
Till our cold and selfish natures,
   Warmed by Thee, at length believe
That more happy and more blessed
   'Tis to give than to receive.

"She cast in all that she had"

Bible Text

God loveth a cheerful giver. — *2 Corinthians 9:7.*

Hymn

Take my silver and my gold,
Not a mite would I withhold;
Take my intellect and use
Every power as Thou shalt choose.

34. The Last Judgment

When the Son of Man shall come in His glory and all the holy angels with Him, then shall He sit upon the throne of His glory; and before Him shall be gathered all nations.[1] And He shall separate them one from another as a shepherd divideth his sheep from the goats; and He shall set the sheep on His right hand, but the goats on the left.

Then shall the King say unto them on His right hand, "Come, ye blessed of My Father, inherit[2] the kingdom prepared for you. For I was an hungered, and ye gave Me meat;[3] I was thirsty, and ye gave me drink; I was a stranger, and ye took Me in; naked, and ye clothed Me; I was sick, and ye visited Me; I was in prison, and ye came unto Me." Then shall the righteous answer Him, "Lord, when saw we Thee an hungered and fed Thee? or thirsty and gave Thee drink? When saw we Thee a stranger and took Thee in? or naked and clothed Thee? Or when saw we Thee sick or in prison and came unto Thee?" And the King shall say, "Inasmuch as ye have done it unto one of the least of these My brethren,[4] ye have done it unto Me."

Then shall He say unto them on the left hand, "Depart from Me, ye cursed, into everlasting fire, prepared for the devil and his angels. For I was an hungered, and ye gave Me no meat; I was thirsty, and ye gave Me no drink; I was a stranger, and ye took Me not in; naked, and ye clothed Me not; sick and in prison, and ye visited Me not."

Then shall they also answer Him, "Lord, when saw we Thee an hungered, or athirst, or a stranger, or naked, or sick, or in prison and did not minister[5] unto Thee?" Then shall He answer them, saying, "Verily, I say unto you, Inasmuch as ye did it not to one of the least of these, ye did it not to Me." And these shall go away into everlasting punishment, but the righteous into life eternal.

Explanatory Notes

[1] All men, the living and the dead. [2] Being My children, receive the share I promised you. [3] Food. [4] Those in need. [5] Serve Thee.

"The Son of Man shall come in His glory"

Bible Text

God hath appointed a day in the which He will judge the world in righteousness by that Man whom He hath ordained. — *Acts 17:31.*

Prayer

Dear Jesus, strengthen our faith and keep us as Thy dear children, that we may be found on Thy right hand in the Judgment. Amen.

35. The Lord's Supper[1]

Jesus said unto His disciples, "Ye know that after two days is the Feast of the Passover,[2] and the Son of Man is betrayed[3] to be crucified."

Then entered Satan into Judas Iscariot,[4] being of the number of the Twelve. And he went unto the chief priests and said, "What will ye give me, and I will deliver Him unto you?"[5]

And they covenanted[6] to give him thirty pieces of silver.[7] From that time he sought opportunity[8] to betray Him.

And Jesus sent Peter and John, saying, "Go and prepare us the Passover that we may eat." And the disciples did as Jesus had appointed[9] them.

Now, when the even[10] was come, He sat down with the Twelve. And He said unto them, "With desire have I desired[11] to eat this passover with you before I suffer."

And as they were eating, Jesus took bread; and when He had given thanks, He brake it and gave it to His disciples and said, "Take, eat; this is My body, which is given for you; this do in remembrance of Me."

After the same manner also He took the cup when He had supped, gave thanks, and gave it to them, saying "Take, drink ye all of it; this cup is the new testament in My blood, which is shed for you for the remission of sins; this do ye, as oft as ye drink it, in remembrance of Me."

Explanatory Notes

[1] This and the following seven stories are an account of the Savior's Passion. They form one continuous story, relating the events which happened from late Thursday afternoon of Holy Week till Saturday evening. [2] The Passover was celebrated on the fourteenth day of the first month, called Nisan. The Passover was also called the Feast of Unleavened Bread. [3] Secretly given up to the enemy. [4] Ju'-das Is-car'-i-ot. [5] I will see that He falls into your hands. [6] Agreed. [7] About $18.75, the price generally paid for a slave at that time. [8] A chance. [9] Told. [10] Evening. [11] I have greatly longed.

"This do in remembrance of Me"

Bible Text

Christ, our Passover, is sacrificed for us. — *1 Corinthians 5:7.*

Hymn

For Thy consoling Supper, Lord,
Be praised throughout all ages.

36. Jesus in Gethsemane[1]

And Jesus went forth[2] over the brook Kidron to the Mount of Olives; and His disciples followed Him. Then said He unto them, "All ye shall be offended[3] because of Me this night." Peter said unto Him, "Though all men shall be offended because of Thee, yet will I never be offended." Jesus said unto him, "Verily I say unto thee. That even in this night, before the cock crow twice, thou shalt deny Me thrice." Then cometh Jesus with them unto Gethsemane; and He taketh with Him Peter and James and John and began to be sorrowful and sore amazed[4] and very heavy;[5] and saith unto them, "My soul is exceeding sorrowful unto death; tarry[6] ye here and watch with Me." And He was withdrawn from them about a stone's cast[7] and fell on His face and prayed, "Abba, Father, all things are possible unto Thee; take this cup[8] from Me; nevertheless not what I will, but what Thou wilt."

And He cometh unto the disciples and findeth them sleeping and saith unto Peter, "Simon, sleepest thou? Watch and pray that ye enter not into temptation; the spirit indeed is willing, but the flesh[9] is weak." He went away the second time and prayed, "O My Father, if this cup may not pass away from Me except I drink it, Thy will be done." And He came and found them asleep again. And He went away again and prayed the third time, saying the same words. And there appeared an angel unto Him from heaven, strengthening Him. And being in an agony,[10] He prayed more earnestly; and His sweat was as it were great drops of blood falling down to the ground.

And when He rose up from prayer and was come to His disciples. He said unto them, "Why sleep ye? Rise up let us go; lo, he that betrayeth Me is at hand."

Explanatory Notes

[1] Geth-sem'-a-ne. [2] From where they had eaten the passover. [3] Fall away. [4] Greatly distressed. [5] Troubled. [6] Wait. [7] As far as one can throw a stone. [8] He compared His suffering with a bitter drink. [9] The sinful heart. [10] Very great suffering, close to death.

"Take this cup from Me!"

Bible Text

Surely He hath borne our griefs and carried our sorrows. — *Isaiah 53:4.*

Hymn

Go to dark Gethsemane, Ye that feel the Tempter's power;
Your Redeemer's conflict see, Watch with Him one bitter hour;
Turn not from His griefs away, Learn of Jesus Christ to pray.

37. The Betrayal of Jesus

And while He yet spake, lo, Judas[1] came and with him a great multitude and officers from the chief priests and Pharisees,[2] with lanterns and torches, with swords and staves.[3] And he that betrayed Him had given them a token,[4] saying, "Whomsoever I shall kiss, that same is He; take Him and lead Him away safely."

Jesus went forth and said unto them, "Whom seek ye?"

They answered Him, "Jesus of Nazareth."[5]

Jesus saith unto them, "I am He."

As soon as He had said unto them, "I am He," they went backward and fell to the ground.

Then asked He them again, "Whom seek ye?"

And they said, "Jesus of Nazareth."

Jesus answered, "I have told you that I am He; if, therefore, ye seek Me, let these[6] go their way."

And forthwith Judas drew near unto Jesus and said, "Hail, Master!" and kissed Him.

And Jesus said unto him, "Friend, wherefore art thou come? Judas, betrayest thou the Son of Man with a kiss?" Then came they and laid hands on Jesus and took Him.

Then Simon Peter, having a sword, drew it and smote[7] the high priest's servant and cut off his right ear.

Then said Jesus unto Peter: "Put up thy sword into the sheath;[8] for all they that take the sword shall perish[9] with the sword. Thinkest thou that I cannot pray to My Father and He shall presently give Me more than twelve legions[10] of angels?" And He touched his[11] ear and healed him.

Then all the disciples forsook[12] Him and fled.

Explanatory Notes

[1] Ju'-das. [2] Phar'-i-sees. [3] Poles or clubs. [4] Sign. [5] Naz'-a-reth. [6] The disciples. [7] Struck. [8] Case for a sword. [9] Die. [10] 60,000 to 72,000. [11] The servant's. [12] Left.

"Hail, Master!"

Bible Text

Yea, Mine own familiar friend, in whom I trusted, which did eat of My bread, hath lifted up his heel against Me. — *Psalm 41:9*.

Prayer

Dear Savior Jesus Christ, help us to be faithful in all things. Keep us from betraying Thee or our fellow men. Hear us for the sake of Thy bitter suffering and death. Amen.

38. Christ Before the High Priest

The band[1] and the officers of the Jews bound Jesus and led him away to Caiaphas,[2] the high priest, where the scribes and the elders all were assembled.

The high priest then asked Jesus of His disciples and of His doctrine.

Jesus answered him, "I spake openly to the world. Ask them which heard Me."

And when He had thus spoken, one of the officers which stood by struck Jesus with the palm of his hand, saying, "Answerest Thou the high priest so?"

Jesus answered him, "If I have spoken evil, bear witness of[3] the evil; but if well, why smitest thou Me?"

Now, the chief priests and elders and all the council[4] sought false witness against Jesus to put Him to death, but found none; yea, though many false witnesses came, yet their witness agreed not together.

And the high priest asked Him and said unto Him, "I adjure[5] Thee by the living God that Thou tell us whether Thou be the Christ, the Son of God."

Jesus saith, "Thou hast said; I am."

Then the high priest rent his clothes, saying, "He hath spoken blasphemy;[6] what further need have we of witnesses?" And they all condemned Him and said, "He is guilty of death."

And the men that held Jesus mocked Him and began to spit in His face and buffeted[7] Him. And when they had blindfolded Him, they struck Him on the face and asked Him, saying, "Prophesy unto us, Thou Christ, who is he that smote Thee?" And many other things blasphemously spake they against Him.

Explanatory Notes

[1] Small troop of soldiers. [2] Ca'-ia-phas. [3] Prove. [4] A body of men called the San'-he-drin, the highest court of the Jewish Church. [5] Put under oath. [6] He has mocked God. [7] Struck Him with their hands or their fists.

"He hath spoken blasphemy!"

Bible Text

I gave My back to the smiters and My cheeks to them that plucked off the hair; I hid not My face from shame and spitting. — *Isaiah 50:6.*

Prayer

Dear Savior, forgive where we have lied or brought false witness against anyone. Make us honest and truthful at all times; for the sake of Thine innocent suffering and death. Amen.

39. Peter's Denial and the Death of Judas

Peter followed Jesus unto the high priest's palace.[1] And the servants and officers had made a fire of coals; and they warmed themselves; and Peter stood with them to see the end.[2] Then saith the damsel[3] that kept the door unto Peter, "Art thou not also one of this Man's disciples?" But he denied before them all, saying, "Woman, I am not."

And after a little while he went out into the porch; and the cock crew.[4] And another maid saw him and said unto them that stood by, "This fellow was also with Jesus of Nazareth." And another said, "Thou art also of them." And again he denied with an oath and said, "Man, I am not; I do not know the Man."

And about the space[5] of an hour after, another confidently affirmed,[6] saying, "Surely thou art one of them; for thou art a Galilean, and thy speech agreeth thereto." [7] One of the servants of the high priest saith, "Did not I see thee in the garden with Him?" Then he began to curse and to sware, saying, "I know not this Man of whom ye speak." And immediately the cock crew the second time.

And the Lord turned and looked upon Peter. And Peter remembered the word that Jesus said unto him, "Before the cock crow twice, thou shalt deny Me thrice." And he went out and wept bitterly.

Then Judas, which had betrayed Jesus, when he saw that He was condemned, repented himself[8] and brought again the thirty pieces of silver to the chief priests and elders, saying, "I have sinned in that I have betrayed innocent blood." And they said, "What is that to us? See thou to that." And he cast down the pieces of silver in the Temple and went and hanged himself; and he burst asunder[9] in the midst, and all his bowels gushed out.[10]

Explanatory Notes

[1] Residence. [2] What would happen to the Lord. [3] Maid.
[4] Crowed. [5] Length. [6] Said, or declared. [7] Gal-i-le'-an; one could hear by Peter's speech that he came from Galilee. [8] Felt sorry. [9] Apart.
[10] The intestines burst out of his body.

"The Lord turned and looked upon Peter"

Bible Text

Godly sorrow worketh repentance to salvation . . . but the sorrow of the world worketh death. — *2 Corinthians 7:10.*

Hymn

In the hour of trial,
Jesus, plead for me
Lest by base denial
I depart from Thee.

40. Christ Before Pilate

And the multitude arose and bound Jesus and delivered Him to Pontius Pilate,[1] the governor. Pilate went out unto them and said, "What accusation[2] bring ye against this man?" They said, "We found this fellow perverting the nation[3] and saying that He is Christ, a king."

Then Pilate asked Jesus, "Art Thou the king of the Jews?" Jesus answered, "My kingdom is not of this world." Pilate said unto Him, "Art Thou a king, then?" Jesus answered, "Thou sayest that I am a king. For this cause came I into the world, that I should bear witness of the truth. Every one that is of the truth heareth My voice."

And Pilate, when he had called together the chief priests and the rulers and the people, said unto them, "I have found no fault in this man. I will therefore chastise[4] Him and release Him." But they cried, "Crucify Him!"

Then Pilate took Jesus and scourged[5] Him. And the soldiers stripped Him and put on Him a scarlet robe and platted[6] a crown of thorns and put it upon His head and a reed[7] in His right hand; and they bowed the knee before Him and smote Him with their hands. And they spit upon Him and took the reed and smote Him on the head.

Pilate went forth again and saith unto them, "Behold, I bring Him forth to you that ye may know that I find no fault in Him." Then came Jesus forth, wearing the crown of thorns and the purple robe. And Pilate saith unto them, "Behold the Man!" When the chief priests and officers saw Him, they cried out, saying, "Crucify Him, crucify Him!"

Pilate took water and washed his hands before the multitude, saying, "I am innocent of the blood of this just person; see ye to it." Then answered all the people and said, "His blood be on us and on our children."

Then delivered he Jesus to their will to be crucified.

Explanatory Notes

[1] Pon'-tius Pi'-late. [2] Charge. [3] Turning the people against the government. [4] Punish. [5] Whipped. [6] Braided. [7] Stick.

"Behold the Man!"

Bible Text

He was wounded for our transgressions, He was bruised for our iniquities; the chastisement of our peace was upon Him, and with His stripes we are healed. — *Isaiah 53:5.*

Prayer

Dear Jesus, we thank Thee that by Thy suffering and death Thou hast saved us from sin, from death, and from the power of the devil. Amen.

41. The Crucifixion of Christ

Then the soldiers of the governor took Jesus and put His own clothes on Him and led Him away to crucify Him; and He, bearing His cross, went forth into a place called Golgotha.

And they crucified Him and two malefactors[1] with Him. And it was the third hour.[2] Then said Jesus, "Father, forgive them; for they know not what they do." When Jesus saw His mother and the disciple standing by whom He loved,[3] He saith unto His mother, "Woman, behold thy son." Then saith He to the disciple, "Behold thy mother." And from that hour that disciple took her unto his own home. And they that passed reviled[4] Him. And one of the malefactors railed[5] on Him, saying, "If Thou be the Christ, save Thyself and us." But the other rebuked him, saying, "This Man hath done nothing amiss."[6] And he said unto Jesus, "Lord, remember me when Thou comest into Thy kingdom." And Jesus said unto him, "Verily I say unto thee, Today shalt thou be with Me in paradise "

Now, from the sixth hour there was darkness over all the land unto the ninth hour. And about the ninth hour Jesus cried with a loud voice, "My God, My God, why hast Thou forsaken Me?"

After this, Jesus, knowing that all things were accomplished, saith, "I thirst." And one of them ran and took a sponge and filled it with vinegar and put it on a reed and gave Him to drink. When Jesus had received the vinegar, He said, "It is finished." And He cried again with a loud voice, "Father, into Thy hands I commend[7] My spirit!" And He bowed His head and gave up the ghost.

And, behold, the veil of the Temple was rent in twain; [8] and the earth did quake, and the rocks rent; and the graves were opened, and many bodies of the saints which slept arose.

Explanatory Notes

[1] Criminals, also called thieves. [2] Nine o'clock in the morning.
[3] John. [4][5] Spoke unkindly. [6] Wrong. [7] Give in charge. [8] Two parts.

"And they crucified Him"

Bible Text

The blood of Jesus Christ, His Son, cleanseth us from all sin. — 1 John 1:7.

Hymn

Through Thy sufferings, death, and merit
I eternal life inherit:
Thousand, thousand thanks shall be,
Dearest Jesus, unto Thee.

42. The Burial of Christ

The Jews, that the bodies should not remain upon the cross on the Sabbath day, besought Pilate that their legs might be broken and that they might be taken away. Then the soldiers brake the legs of the first and of the other which was crucified with Him. But when they came to Jesus and saw that He was dead already, they brake not His legs, but one of the soldiers with a spear pierced His side, and forthwith came there out blood and water.

And when the even was come, there came Joseph of Arimathea,[1] an honorable counselor, who had not consented to the counsel and deed of them,[2] being a disciple of Jesus, but secretly for fear of the Jews, and begged the body of Jesus. Pilate commanded the body to be delivered. There came also Nicodemus[3] and brought a mixture of myrrh and aloes.[4] Then took they the body of Jesus and wound it in linen clothes with the spices.

Now there was a garden and in the garden a new sepulcher,[5] hewn out of a rock. There laid they Jesus and rolled a great stone to the door of the sepulcher and departed. And Mary Magdalene[6] and other women beheld where He was laid. And they returned and prepared spices and ointments; and rested the Sabbath day.

Now, the next day the chief priests and Pharisees came together unto Pilate, saying: "Sir, we remember that that deceiver said while He was yet alive, 'After three days I will rise again.' Command therefore that the sepulcher be made sure until the third day, lest His disciples come by night and steal Him away and say to the people, 'He is risen from the dead.'" Pilate said unto them, "Ye have a watch; go your way; make it as sure as ye can." So they made the sepulcher sure, sealing the stone and setting a watch.

Explanatory Notes

[1] Ar-i-ma-the'-a. [2] Had not, like the others, condemned Jesus to death. [3] Nic-o-de'-mus, also a secret disciple of Jesus. John 3:1ff. [4] Used for embalming, very expensive. [5] Grave. [6] Mary Mag'-da-lene, out of whom He had cast seven devils. Mark 16:9.

"There laid they Jesus"

Bible Text

The Son of Man must be delivered into the hands of sinful men and be crucified, and the third day rise again. — *Luke 24:7.*

Hymn

Jesus, crucified for me,
Is my Life, my hope's Foundation,
And my Glory and Salvation.

43. The Resurrection of Christ

And when the Sabbath day was passed, Mary Magdalene[1] and Mary, the mother of James, and Salome,[2] had bought sweet spices that they might come and anoint Him. And very early in the morning, the first day of the week, they came unto the sepulcher[3] at the rising of the sun.

And, behold, there was a great earthquake; for the angel of the Lord descended from heaven and came and rolled back the stone from the door and sat upon it. His countenance[4] was like lightning and his raiment[5] white as snow. And for fear of him the keepers did shake and became as dead men.

And the women said among themselves, "Who shall roll us away the stone from the door of the sepulcher?" And when they looked, they saw that the stone was rolled away. When Mary Magdalene seeth the stone taken away, she runneth and cometh to Simon Peter and to the other disciple, whom Jesus loved, and saith unto them, "They have taken away the Lord out of the sepulcher, and we know not where they have laid Him."

The women, entering into the sepulcher, saw a young man sitting on the right-hand side, clothed in a long, white garment; and they were affrighted.[6] And the angel said unto them, "Be not affrighted; for I know ye seek Jesus of Nazareth,[7] which was crucified. He is not here, for He is risen as He hath said. Come and see the place where the Lord lay. And go quickly and tell His disciples and Peter that He is risen from the dead. And, behold, He goeth before you into Galilee;[8] there shall ye see Him."

And they went out quickly and fled from the sepulcher with fear and great joy.

Explanatory Notes

[1] Mag'-da-lene. [2] Sa-lo'-me, the mother of James the Elder and John. [3] Grave. [4] Face. [5] Clothing. [6] Afraid. [7] Naz'-a-reth. [8] Gal'-i-lee.

"He is risen, as He hath said"

Bible Text

He was declared to be the Son of God with power, according to the Spirit of holiness, by the resurrection from the dead. — *Romans 1:4.*

Hymn

He lives; all glory to His name!
He lives, my Jesus, still the same.
Oh, the sweet joy this sentence gives,
"I know that my Redeemer lives"!

44. The First Appearances of the Risen Lord

But Mary stood without at the sepulcher,[1] weeping. And she saw Jesus standing and knew not that it was Jesus. Jesus saith unto her, "Woman, why weepest thou? Whom seekest thou?"

She, supposing Him to be the gardener, saith unto Him, "Sir, if thou hast borne[2] Him hence, tell me where thou hast laid Him."

Jesus saith unto her, "Mary!"

She turned herself and saith unto Him, "Rabboni!" [3] which is to say, Master.

Jesus saith unto her, "Touch Me not; for I am not yet ascended to My Father; but go to My brethren and say unto them, 'I ascend unto My Father and your Father, and to My God and your God.'"

Mary Magdalene[4] came and told the disciples that she had seen the Lord and that He had spoken these things.

And as the other women went to tell His disciples, behold, Jesus met them, saying, "All hail!" [5] And they came and held Him by the feet and worshiped Him.

Then said Jesus unto them, "Be not afraid; go and tell My brethren that they go into Galilee,[6] and there shall they see Me."

Now, when they were going, some of the watch came into the city and showed unto the chief priests all the things that were done. And when they were assembled with the elders and had taken counsel,[7] they gave large money unto the soldiers, saying, "Say ye, 'His disciples came by night and stole Him away while we slept.' And if this come to the governor's ears, we will persuade[8] him and secure[9] you."

So they took the money and did as they were taught.

Explanatory Notes

[1] Grave. [2] Carried. [3] Rab-bo'-ni. [4] Mag'-da-lene. [5] A friendly greeting. [6] Gal'-i-lee. [7] Had talked it over. [8] Satisfy, perhaps by paying him a bribe. [9] Protect.

"Woman, why weepest thou?"

Bible Text

If Christ be not raised, your faith is vain; ye are yet in your sins. — *1 Corinthians 15:17.*

Hymn

Jesus, my Redeemer, lives;
I, too, unto life shall waken.

45. Christ Appears to His Disciples

The same day,[1] at evening, being the first day of the week, when the doors were shut where the disciples were assembled for fear of the Jews, came Jesus and stood in the midst and saith unto them, "Peace be unto you!"

But they were terrified and affrighted[2] and supposed that they had seen a spirit.

And He said unto them, "Why are ye troubled? And why do thoughts arise in your hearts? Behold My hands and My feet that it is I Myself; handle[3] Me and see; for a spirit hath not flesh and bones as ye see Me have." And when He had thus spoken, He showed them His hands and His feet.

Then were the disciples glad when they saw the Lord. Then said Jesus unto them again: "Peace be unto you! As My Father hath sent Me, even so send I you." And when He had said this, He breathed on them and saith unto them, "Receive ye the Holy Ghost; whosesoever sins ye remit,[4] they are remitted unto them; and whosesoever sins ye retain,[5] they are retained."

Then the eleven disciples went away into Galilee,[6] into a mountain where Jesus had appointed[7] them. And when they saw Him, they worshiped Him; but some doubted. And Jesus came and spake unto them, saying, "All power is given unto Me in heaven and in earth. Go ye, therefore, and teach all nations, baptizing them in the name of the Father and of the Son and of the Holy Ghost; teaching them to observe[8] all things whatsoever I have commanded you. He that believeth and is baptized shall be saved, but he that believeth not shall be damned. And, lo, I am with you alway, even unto the end of the world." [9]

Explanatory Notes

[1] Easter Sunday, on which Jesus had risen. [2] Very much afraid. [3] Touch and feel. [4] Forgive. [5] Do not forgive. [6] Gal'-i-lee. [7] Directed, told. [8] Do and keep. [9] This is Christ's great command to all Christians to teach and preach the Gospel.

"Go ye, therefore, and teach all nations"

Bible Text

Blessed are they that have not seen and yet have believed. — *John 20:29.*

Hymn

Salvation, O salvation!
The joyful sound proclaim
Till each remotest nation
Has learned Messiah's name.

46. The Ascension[1] of Christ

Jesus showed Himself alive after His Passion[2] by many infallible proofs,[3] being seen of His disciples forty days and speaking of the things pertaining to the kingdom of God.[4] And being assembled together with them, He said unto them, "Behold, I send the promise of My Father upon you; but tarry[5] ye in the city of Jerusalem[6] until ye be endued with[7] power from on high. For John truly baptized with water; but ye shall be baptized with the Holy Ghost not many days hence."

So, then, after the Lord had spoken unto them, He led them out as far as to Bethany;[8] and He lifted up His hands and blessed them. And it came to pass, while He blessed them, He was parted from them and carried up into heaven; and a cloud received Him out of their sight; and He sat on the right hand of God.[9]

And while they looked steadfastly[10] toward heaven as He went up, behold, two men stood by them in white apparel,[11] which also said, "Ye men of Galilee,[12] why stand ye gazing up into heaven? This same Jesus which is taken up from you into heaven shall so come in like manner as ye have seen Him go into heaven."[13]

And they worshiped Him and returned to Jerusalem with great joy.

Explanatory Notes

[1] Going into heaven. [2] After His suffering and death. [3] Proofs that are absolutely certain. The resurrection of Jesus is sure; it cannot be denied. [4] He taught them many things that they needed to know in order to carry on His work after He would be gone. [5] Stay. [6] Je-ru'-sa-lem. [7] Until you receive, or are filled with. [8] Beth'-a-ny. [9] The meaning of the statement that Jesus sits at the right hand of God is that He rules over all things together with the Father and the Holy Ghost. [10] Steadily and continually. [11] Clothes. [12] Gal'-i-lee. [13] Jesus will return visibly on Judgment Day, even as He ascended visibly.

Hail the day that sees Him rise
To His throne above the skies!

"He was parted from them"

Bible Text

Where I am, there shall also My servant be. — *John 12:26.*

Hymn

Draw us to Thee, for then shall we
Walk in Thy steps forever
And hasten on where Thou art gone
To be with Thee, dear Savior.

47. Pentecost

And when the day of Pentecost[1] was fully come, they were all with one accord[2] in one place. And suddenly there came a sound from heaven as of a rushing, mighty wind, and it filled all the house where they were sitting. And there appeared unto them cloven tongues as of fire,[3] and it sat upon each of them. And they were all filled with the Holy Ghost and began to speak with other tongues[4] as the Spirit gave them utterance.[5] And there were dwelling at Jerusalem, Jews, devout[6] men, out of every nation under heaven. Now, when this was noised abroad,[7] the multitude came together, and they were all amazed and marveled, saying: "Behold, are not all these which speak Galileans?[8] And how hear we every man speak in our own tongue the wonderful works of God?" Others, mocking, said, "These men are full of new wine."

But Peter, standing up with the Eleven, lifted up his voice and said unto them: "Ye men of Israel, hear these words: Jesus of Nazareth, a Man approved of God[9] among you by miracles, Him ye have crucified and slain; whom God hath raised up, whereof we all are witnesses. Therefore let all the house of Israel know assuredly that God hath made that same Jesus whom ye have crucified both Lord and Christ."

Now, when they heard this, they were pricked in their hearts[10] and said, "Men and brethren, what shall we do?" Then Peter said unto them, "Repent and be baptized in the name of Jesus Christ for the remission of sins, and ye shall receive the gift of the Holy Ghost." Then they that gladly received His word were baptized; and the same day there were added unto them about three thousand souls.

Explanatory Notes

[1] Pentecost means fiftieth; it was celebrated fifty days after the Passover; see Leviticus 23. [2] In perfect agreement. [3] Flames of fire in the form of split tongues. [4] Languages. [5] Moved them to speak. [6] Very religious. [7] Heard by the people. [8] Gal-i-le'-ans. [9] God was perfectly satisfied with Him. [10] Touched and moved to repentance.

"Repent and be baptized in the name of Jesus Christ"

Bible Text

And it shall come to pass afterward that I will pour out My Spirit upon all flesh. — *Joel 2:28.*

Hymn

Holy Ghost, with light divine
Shine upon this heart of mine;
Chase the shades of night away;
Turn the darkness into day.

48. The Healing of the Lame Man

Now, Peter and John went up together into the Temple at the hour of prayer, being the ninth hour.[1] And a certain lame man was laid daily at the gate of the Temple to ask alms[2] of them that entered into the Temple; who, seeing Peter and John about to go into the Temple, asked an alms.

And Peter said, "Look on us."

And he gave heed[3] unto them, expecting to receive something of them.

Then Peter said, "Silver and gold have I none; but such as I have give I thee: in the name of Jesus Christ of Nazareth[4] rise up and walk." And he took him by the right hand and lifted him up; and immediately he stood and walked and entered with them into the Temple, walking and leaping and praising God. And all the people saw him walking and praising God. And as the healed man held[5] Peter and John, all the people ran together unto them.

And when Peter saw it, he answered unto the people: "Ye men of Israel,[6] why marvel ye at this,[7] or why look ye so earnestly on us as though by our own power we had made this man to walk? The God of Abraham[8] and Isaac[9] and of Jacob[10] hath glorified His Son Jesus, whom ye delivered up and denied Him in the presence of Pilate. But ye denied the Holy One and the Just and desired a murderer[11] to be granted unto you, and killed the Prince of Life, whom God hath raised from the dead; whereof we are witnesses. I wot[12] that through ignorance ye did it, as did also your rulers. Repent ye, therefore, and be converted,[13] that your sins may be blotted out." [14]

And many of them which heard the word believed; and the number of men was five thousand.

Explanatory Notes

[1] Three o'clock in the afternoon. [2] Gifts. [3] Attention. [4] Naz'-a-reth. [5] Clung to, or remained with. [6] Is'-ra-el. [7] Why are you so surprised? [8] A'-bra-ham. [9] I'-saac. [10] Ja'-cob. [11] Bar-ab'-bas. [12] Know. [13] Changed into believers. [14] Forgiven.

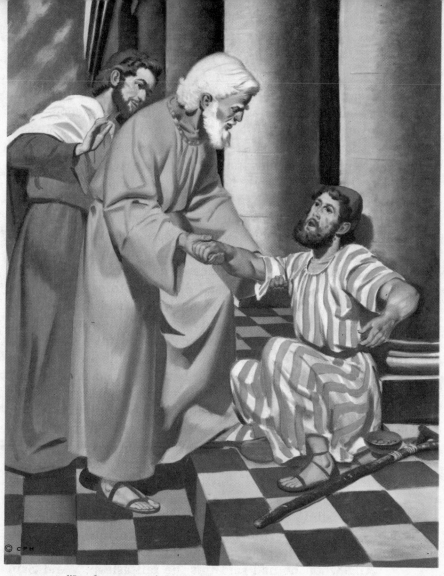

"In the name of Jesus Christ rise up and walk"

Bible Text

And these signs shall follow them that believe . . . they shall lay hands on the sick, and they shall recover. — *Mark 16:17-18.*

Prayer

Lord Jesus, Thine is the kingdom and the power and the glory forever. Give us the faith to accept Thee joyfully as our Savior. Amen.

49. Stephen

Stephen,[1] full of faith, did great miracles among the people. Then there arose certain of the synagog,[2] disputing[3] with Stephen. And they were not able to resist[4] the wisdom and the spirit by which he spake. And they stirred up the people and set up false witnesses, which said, "This man ceaseth not to speak blasphemous words against this holy place[5] and the Law; for we have heard him say that this Jesus of Nazareth shall destroy this place and shall change the customs[6] which Moses delivered us." And all that sat in the council, looking steadfastly on him, saw his face as it had been the face of an angel.

Then said the high priest, "Are these things so?" And he said: "Ye stiff-necked and uncircumcised in heart and ears; [7] as your fathers did, so do ye. Which of the prophets have not your fathers persecuted? [8] And they have slain them which showed before[9] of the coming of the Just One, of whom ye have been now the betrayers and murderers."

When they heard these things, they gnashed on him with their teeth.[10] But he, being full of the Holy Ghost, looked up steadfastly into heaven and said, "Behold, I see the heavens opened and the Son of Man standing on the right hand of God." Then they cast him out of the city. And the witnesses laid down their clothes[11] at a young man's feet, whose name was Saul. And they stoned Stephen, calling upon God and saying, "Lord Jesus, receive my spirit!" And he kneeled down and cried with a loud voice, "Lord, lay not this sin to their charge!"

And when he had said this, he fell asleep. And Saul was consenting unto[12] his death. And devout men carried Stephen to his burial.

Explanatory Notes

[1] Ste'-phen, one of the seven deacons of the congregation in Jerusalem. [2] Members of the Jewish Council. [3] Arguing. [4] Stand up against. [5] The Temple. [6] Laws. [7] Wicked who refuse to repent. [8] Made life miserable for them and even killed them. [9] Foretold. [10] Because they were very angry. [11] Outer garments. [12] Pleased with.

"They stoned Stephen"

Bible Text

These are they which came out of great tribulation and have washed their robes and made them white in the blood of the Lamb. — *Revelation 7:14.*

Prayer

Gracious Lord, grant us a blessed death when our last hour is at hand. Hear us for Jesus' sake. Amen.

50. The Conversion of Saul

And Saul, breathing out threatenings and slaughter[1] against the disciples of the Lord, went to the high priest and desired of him letters to Damascus, to the synagogs, that if he found any of this way,[2] he might bring them bound to Jerusalem.[3] And as he came near Damascus,[4] suddenly there shined round about him a light from heaven. And he fell to the earth and heard a voice saying unto him, "Saul, Saul, why persecutest thou Me?" And he said, "Who art Thou, Lord?" And the Lord said, "I am Jesus, whom thou persecutest." And he, trembling and astonished, said, "Lord, what wilt Thou have me to do?" And the Lord said, "Arise and go into the city, and it shall be told thee what thou must do." And Saul arose; and when his eyes were opened, he saw no man; but they led him by the hand and brought him into Damascus.

And there was a disciple at Damascus named Ananias.[5] To him said the Lord in a vision:[6] "Ananias, inquire in the house of Judas for Saul of Tarsus;[7] for, behold, he prayeth. He is to bear My name before the Gentiles[8] and kings and the children of Israel." And Ananias went and entered into the house, and, putting his hands on him, said, "Brother Saul, the Lord, even Jesus, hath sent me that thou mightest receive thy sight and be filled with the Holy Ghost." And he received sight and arose and was baptized.

Then Saul was certain days with the disciples at Damascus. And straightway he preached Christ in the synagogs, that He is the Son of God. And the Jews took counsel[9] to kill him; and they watched the gates day and night. Then the disciples took him by night and let him down by the wall in a basket. And when Saul was come to Jerusalem, he spake boldly in the name of the Lord Jesus.

Explanatory Notes

[1] He was fierce in persecuting and killing. [2] Believers in Christ. [3] Je-ru'-sa-lem. [4] Da-mas'-cus. [5] An-a-ni'-as. [6] The Lord appeared to him. [7] Tar'-sus. [8] Those not Jewish. [9] Met to discuss the matter.

"He fell to the earth and heard a voice"

Bible Text

The wolf shall dwell with the lamb, and the leopard shall lie down with the kid. — *Isaiah 11:6.*

Prayer

Merciful God, break and hinder the evil plans of those who hate Thee, and turn their hearts to faith in Thee; for Jesus' sake. Amen.

PRONUNCIATIONS OF PROPER NAMES

KEY TO THE SIGNS USED

Sʏʟʟᴀʙʟᴇs are indicated by a hyphen (-), while those on which stress has to be laid are marked with an accent (′).

ā	*as in*	dāy.	ẽ	*as in*	tẽrm.
ē	”	mēte.	ĩ	”	fĩrm.
ī	”	tīme.	ô	”	lôrd.
ō	”	ōld.	û	”	tûrn.
ū	”	ūse.	ṳ	”	rṳde.
ȳ	”	defȳ.	āi	”	aid.
a̍	”	sena̍te.	ew̄	”	Jew̄s.
e̍	”	e̍vent.	oi	”	oil.
i̍	”	i̍dea.	aō	”	Pharaōh.
o̍	”	o̍bey.	ç	=	s (Sadduçees).
u̍	”	u̍nite.	ꞓ,ꞓh	=	k (Ꞓain; Ꞓhaldea).
ă	”	ădd.	ġ	=	j (Ġentile).
ĕ	”	ĕnd.	ḡ	*as in*	ḡet (Ḡethsemane).
ĭ	”	ĭll.	ị	=	y (Christịan).
ŏ	”	nŏt.	ṣ	=	z (Moṣeṣ).
ŭ	”	ŭs.	x̣	=	gz (Alex̣andria).
y̆	”	pity̆.	t̲h̲	=	t (T̲h̲omas).
â	”	câre.	c̲i̲	=	sh, shi (Cilic̲i̲a).
ä	”	fär.	t̲i̲	=	sh, shi (Egypt̲i̲an).
ȧ	”	lȧst.	s̲i̲	=	sh, shi (Pers̲i̲a).
a̤	”	fa̤ll.			

Pronunciations

Aår'ŏn

Ăb'bå

Ă-bĕd'nĕ-gō

Ā'bĕl

Ā'bră-hăm

Ăb'să-lŏm

Ăd'ăm

Ā'hăb

Ăm'ă-lĕk

Ăm'ă-lĕk-ītes

Ăm'mŏn

Ăm'mŏn-ītes

Ăm'ô-rītes

Ăn-å-nī'ăs

Ăn'drēw

Ăr'å-răt

Ăr-ĭ-må-thē'å

Ăsh'ēr

Ạu-gŭstus

Bā'-ăl

Bā'bĕl

Băb'-ў-lŏn

Băp'tĭst

Băth-shē'bå

Bē'lĭ-ăl

Bĕn'jă-mĭn

Bĕth'å-nў

Bĕth'ĕl

Bĕth'lĕ-hĕm

Bĕth'lĕ-hĕm-
    īte

Bĕth'phå-gĕ

Bō'ăz

Çae'şår

Çā'ịå-phăs

Çāin

Çā-ī'năn

Çā'lĕb

Çā'nā

Çā'năan

Çā'năan-ītes

Çå-pēr'nå-ŭm

Çhăl-dē'ăns

Çhē'rĭth

Çhĭl'ĭ-ŏn

Çhrīst

Çў-rē'nĭ-ŭs

Dā'gŏn

Då-măs'cŭs

Dăn

Dăn'ịel

Då-rī'ŭs

Dā'vĭd

Dĕ-lī'låh

Ē'dĕn

Ē'gўpt

E-gўp'tịăn

Ē'lī

E-lī'ăs

E-lī'jăh

E-lĭm'ĕ-lĕch

E-lĭş'å-bĕth

E-lī'shå

Ĕl'kă-nåh

Ē'nŏch

Ē'nŏs

E-şā'ịăs

Ē'sạu

Ēve

Gā'brĭ-ĕl

Găd

Găd'å-rēneş

Găl'ĭ-lēe

Gā'zå

Gē̆-hā'zī

Gĕn-nĕs'å-rĕt

Gĕn'tīles

Gēr'gĕ-sēneş

Gĕth-sĕm'å-nĕ

Gĭd'ĕ-ŏn

Gŏl'gŏ-thå

Gô-lī'ăth

Gô-mŏr'råh

Grēek

Hăm

Hăn'nåh

Hē'brēw

Hē'brŏn

Hĕr'ŏd

Hĕ-rō'dĭ-ăs

Hō'lў Ghōst

Hō'rĕb

Hô-săn'nå

I'şăac

Ĭs-căr'ĭ-ŏt

Ĭsh'må-ĕl-ītes

Ĭş'rå-ĕl

Ĭş'rå-ĕl-ītes

Ĭs'så-chär

Jā'bĕsh

Jā'eŏb

Jå-ī'rŭs

Jămeş

Jā'phĕth

Jă'rĕd	Măg'-dȧ-lēne	Nō'ȧh	Săm'sŏn
Jĕr'ĭ-ehō	Mȧ-hā'lȧ-lē-ĕl	Ō'bĕd	Săm'ū-ĕl
Jĕ-ru̯'sȧ-lĕm	Mäh'lŏn	Ol'ĭveṣ	Săn'hĕ-drĭn
Jĕs'sĕ	Mȧ-nō'ȧh	Ôr'päh	Sā'rȧh
Jē-ṣu̯s	Mär'thȧ		Sā'tăn
Jēws	Mȧ'rў	Pĕ-nĭn'nȧh	Sau̯l
Jĕz'ĕ-bĕl	Mē'shăeh	Pĕn'tĕ-cŏst	Sĕth
Jĕz'rĕ-ĕl	Mĕs-sī'ăs	Pē'tĕr	Shā'drăeh
Jō'ăb	Mĕ-thū'sĕ-lȧh	Phā'raōh	Shē'ehĕm
Jŏhn	Mĭd'ĭ-ăn	Phar'ĭ-sēe	Shĕm
Jŏr'dăn	Mĭd'ĭ-ăn-ītes	Phĭl'ĭp	Sī'dŏn
Jō'sĕph	Mō'ăb	Phĭ-lĭs'tĭneṣ	Sĭm'ĕ-ŏn
Jŏsh'ū-ȧ	Mŏ-rī'ȧh	Pī'lăte	Sī'mŏn
Ju̯'dȧ	Mō'ṣĕṣ	Pŏn'ţiŭs	Sī'naī
Ju̯'dȧh		Pŏt'ĭ-phȧr	Sŏd'ŏm
Ju̯'dȧs	Nā'ȧ-măn		Sŏl'ŏ-mŏn
Ju̯-dē'ȧ	Nā'bŏth	Răb'bȧh	Stē'phĕn
	Nā'ĭn	Răb'bī	Sў̆r'ĭ-ȧ
Kĭd'rŏn	Nȧ-ō'mī	Răb-bō'nī	
Kĭsh	Năph'tȧ-lī	Rā'chĕl	Tär'sŭs
Kī'shŏn	Nā'thăn	Rĕ-bĕk'ȧh	Ĭʼm'năth
	Nȧ-thăn'ȧ-ĕl	Reu̯'bĕn	Tў̄re
Lā'băn	Năz'ȧ-rĕth	Rō'măns	
Lā'mĕeh	Năz'ȧ-rīte	Ru̯th	Ŭ-rī'ȧh
Lăz'ȧ-rŭs	Nē'bō		
Lē'ȧh	Nĕb-û-ehăd-	Sȧ-lō'mĕ	Zăe-ehaē'ŭs
Lē'vī	nĕz'-zȧr	Sȧ-mā'rĭ-ȧ	Zăch-ȧ-rī'ȧs
Lē'vīte	Nĭe-ŏ-dē'mŭs	Sȧ-măr'ĭ-tăn	Zăr'ĕ-phăth
Lŏt			Zĕb'û-lŭn